SPIRALING UP

COMMAND YOUR LIGHT!

KAREN RUDOLF

You can exhale here. Nothing is required.

The Spiral Invocation

(For opening)

I am the light I once longed to find.
The whisper I once sought to hear.
No longer asking — I am becoming.
No longer waiting — I am alive in motion.

I speak with the voice of creation itself,
commanding frequency with grace and gratitude.
Every fall, every rise, a spiral upward —
each breath, a bridge between heaven and earth.

I am remembrance in motion,
love embodied, awakening potential in others to rise too.

— **Karen Rudolf**

Table of Contents

Foreword

Reverend Dr. Alma Stevens

There are moments in life when we meet a soul whose very presence is a reminder that healing is not only possible—it is our birthright. Karen Rudolf is such a soul. Her life, her work, and her light have been a testament to what unfolds when someone listens deeply, surrenders courageously, and walks forward with a heart willing to serve.

When Karen asked me to write this foreword, I paused—not out of hesitation, but out of reverence. I knew this book was not simply the next step in her career. It was the expression of a lifelong conversation between her spirit and the Divine... a conversation she now offers to you.

It is important to say clearly:
This is not just Karen's story.
This is a guide for your transformation.

Spiraling UP: Command Your Light! is more than a book. It is an invitation into remembrance—of your resilience, your intuition, your capacity to rise, and the light you were born carrying.

Karen teaches not from theory but from lived experience—moments where life's storms became teachers, where pain became a portal, and where faith was not something she reached for, but something she recognized had been within her all along.

What I have always admired about Karen is her devotion to truth. She does not shy away from the shadows, nor does she pretend that rising is effortless. Instead, she guides us with compassion, humor, and profound clarity, showing us that the spiral upward is not linear but sacred. Each turn brings us closer to who we truly are.

In these pages, you will not only witness Karen's evolution—you will feel your own awakening begin. You will be invited to slow down, to listen more deeply, and to remember the light you are made of. Through her Butterfly Technique, her stories, and her embodied wisdom, you will discover that every setback is secretly a setup for expansion.

This book is a companion for the seeker, the healer, the weary, and the ready. It is a mirror for the part of you that senses there is more— more love, more purpose, more truth waiting to rise within you.

I am honored to witness Karen's becoming, and even more honored that you now get to experience the essence of her wisdom. May these pages uplift you, comfort you, challenge you, and ultimately remind you of your own inner radiance.

As you read, may you feel the Divine whispering through each line...

Rise. Remember. Reclaim the light you command.

— Reverend Dr. Alma Stevens

Introduction

The Spiral Isn't a Detour — It's the Design

What if the thing you've been calling "backsliding" is actually your *next level* attempting to break through?

Because here's what I've noticed after years of supporting high-capacity humans: growth rarely shows up like a straight line. It shows up like a spiral. You revisit an old trigger... with new awareness. You meet the same fear... with stronger legs underneath you. You face a familiar choice... and this time, you choose yourself.

That's spiraling up.

And if you've been living with the quiet sense that you were made for more—not more *busy*, but more *truth*, more *freedom*, more *alignment*—this book is for you.

Why this book exists

We're living in a time where so many people are outwardly "fine," yet inwardly running on fumes. Visionary leaders, entrepreneurs, creatives, caregivers, builders—people who carry a lot—often master external performance while privately managing internal pressure.

And pressure has a way of getting loud.

It can show up as overthinking, self-doubt, reactivity, people-pleasing, exhaustion, inflammation, strained communication, or that familiar feeling of "I don't even recognize myself right now." Sometimes it shows up as success that looks impressive... yet doesn't feel fulfilling.

This book isn't here to diagnose you. It's here to remind you: ***you are not broken—you are becoming.***

What you'll learn here

Spiraling Up: Command Your Light! is a guide for the moments when life cracks you open... and asks you to lead from a deeper place.

Inside these pages, you'll learn how to:

> Recognize when you're operating from old programming (even when it looks "productive")

> Shift your internal dialogue so your words stop working against you

> Restore capacity when you're depleted—without needing to disappear from your life to do it

> Use simple practices to regulate your nervous system and access clarity faster

> Reclaim your voice, your standards, and your next right step

> Lead—at home, in relationships, in business, and in your own mind—from a new paradigm

This isn't about "think positive and push through."
It's about *changing what you're creating from.*

Why you can trust this process

I didn't write this from theory alone.

I've spent years studying and practicing modalities that support real, lasting transformation—mind-body coherence, subconscious repatterning, trauma-informed approaches, and communication that restores integrity from the inside out. I've also had the honor of hosting deep conversations with leaders and change-makers who remind us that awakening isn't a concept—it's a lived experience.

Most importantly, I've lived the spiral myself: the breakdowns that became breakthroughs, the moments that forced me to listen differently, lead differently, and choose myself differently.

This book is a distillation of what works when life is real and you still have to show up.

How this book is structured

Think of this book as a pathway you can walk in order—or return to whenever life invites you back to a familiar lesson.

You'll move through a progression that looks something like this:

Awareness — noticing your patterns without shaming yourself for having them

Regulation — stabilizing your inner world so you can choose your response

Reframe + Release — shifting the story, softening the grip of the past

Aligned Action — taking steps that match who you're becoming

Embodied Leadership — living from the light you command, not the fear you inherited

Some chapters will feel like a warm hand on your shoulder. Others might feel like a loving mirror. A few may feel like a gentle shove (the good kind). And yes—if you get a little emotionally spicy at times, congratulations: you're alive and doing the work.

How to use this book

You can read it straight through, or you can let it meet you where you are.

Here's a simple rhythm that works beautifully:

>   **Read** one section with curiosity

>   **Pause** and notice what your body feels (your body is always communicating)

>   **Journal** a few honest lines—nothing fancy

>   **Choose** one small step of change

>   **Repeat** when life loops you back around (because it will... and that's not a failure)

Spiraling up doesn't require perfection.
It requires presence.

A gentle note about the world we live in

Some of the experiences that shape our inner world are deeply personal—and some are painfully widespread. That's not just a statistic—it's a reminder that many people are carrying stories their nervous systems never got to complete.

So if any part of this book touches tender territory, go slowly. Be kind to yourself. Get support when you need it. Strength isn't "handling it alone." Strength is honoring your humanity.

The invitation

As you begin, I want to offer you this truth:

The light you command isn't something you earn. It's something you remember.
It's already in you—beneath the noise, beneath the old narratives, beneath the urgency.

This book is an invitation back to that place.

Take a breath.
Let your shoulders drop.
And turn the page.

— Karen Rudolf

www.TranquilSOULutions.com

The Awakening Within

---

*"Awakening isn't something that happens once—
it's the moment you decide to listen again."*
— **Karen Rudolf**

The Opening & Early Knowing

From the time I can remember, I always felt a quiet knowing inside me—something that didn't need to be explained, only trusted. It would rise like warmth in my chest or a soft hum behind the noise of the world. I wouldn't have called it intuition then; at five years old, it was simply the way life whispered to me.

When my parents fought, the air in the house grew heavy and sharp. I'd slip out the door, my small feet carrying me down the street to a secret place that felt like magic. There, beneath an old shrub shaped like an igloo, I'd crawl inside and breathe again. It was my sanctuary—green, still, and somehow safe.

I'd bring my dolls and a handful of leaves, pretending I was healing them from invisible aches. I didn't know how I knew, only that I did. The leaves were medicine, my hands channels of comfort, my imagination the first language of Spirit. That hidden shrub became the place where I first heard life's quiet hum and learned that peace wasn't something found out there; it lived inside me.

Even then, before I had words for it, I was learning the sacred balance between being and doing. Inside that little green cocoon, there was nothing to fix or chase—only the quiet experience of being. That stillness would become my first teacher, though it would take years before I understood its wisdom.

As I grew older, I started noticing how often that same knowing appeared. It nudged me in small ways—a whisper, a tingle, a sense of déjà vu that I couldn't explain. It was never dramatic; it was gentle, steady, and sure.

When I began finishing my boyfriend's sentences before he said them, my "knowing" no longer felt like a gift; it startled him. He laughed at first, then his laughter turned uneasy.

"Could you not do that? You're starting to freak me out!" he said one day. Though he was trying to smile, his eyes told me he was unsettled.

I remember the sting of that moment—the confusion that what felt natural to me could make someone else uncomfortable. No one around me ever talked about intuition, energy, or unseen connection, so I assumed it was something to hide. Maybe there was something wrong with me, I thought.

And so, piece by piece, I turned it off. I stopped listening. I ignored the nudges, sensations, and inner voice that had once felt like home.

For years, I lived that way—disconnected from my own compass, trying to fit into a world that preferred logic to knowing. Vulnerability felt unsafe then. I thought strength meant silence.

Silencing our truth doesn't make it disappear—it only drives it deeper. The more I ignored my intuition, the more disconnected I became from myself, mistaking busyness for purpose and movement for direction.

At first, the silence seemed like peace. And in truth, it was absence— the quiet ache of losing a part of myself I couldn't name.

The Science of Childhood Knowing

Neuroscience shows that children naturally access *interoception* and *neuroception*—the body's built-in system for sensing emotional truth and energetic shifts before the mind creates language to describe them. Your early "knowing" wasn't imaginary. It was your nervous system reading reality clearly and intuitively.

THE SILENCE — TURNING OFF THE INTUITION

As the world began to shape me, I learned to prioritize logic over instinct. Approval over alignment. Predictability over presence. My intuition didn't disappear; it simply receded into the background, waiting patiently for my return.

And losing that inner knowing came at a cost. The stillness I once found under the shrub was replaced by striving. The hum I listened to as a child became buried beneath responsibility.

What I didn't understand then was that intuition doesn't vanish.
It waits.
It whispers.
And eventually—it calls you back.

Why We Shut Down Intuition

We mute intuition for one of three reasons:

(1) to fit in,
(2) to feel safe,
(3) to avoid being "too much."
The brain prioritizes belonging over authenticity, so we learn to tune out the very guidance that once kept us aligned.

Reconnection

It took years for life to circle back and remind me who I was.

By then, I was deep in the rhythm of responsibilities—six hours a day of carpooling to three different schools, managing a house, riding my horse, and juggling after-school activities while holding myself together through a divorce. I kept my focus on what had to be done, not on what was quietly undone inside me.

I prayed constantly for strength. "Dear God, just a little more," I whispered on endless drives, as if endurance alone would make me whole.

Then one afternoon, as I exited the highway, a voice on the radio cut through my thoughts:

"The more we pray for strength, the more challenges we receive."

The words stopped me cold.

Ouch, I thought.

I'd been asking for the wrong thing. Right there at a red light, I changed my prayer: Give me wisdom instead.

That single shift opened a doorway.

The moment I stopped striving for strength and opened to wisdom, I began to see how 'being' births the right thing to do. I didn't need to push through; I needed to align. Alignment, I would later learn, is the true currency of success—not effort or hustle, rather harmony between intention and action.

Why "Wisdom" Activates Transformation

Praying for strength engages survival mode.

Praying for wisdom engages the prefrontal cortex—the decision-making, intuitive, visionary part of the brain.

Wisdom elevates you into clarity, not resistance.

Soon after, at a Spiritual Creativity Conference, life sent me Joe Mínguez. His jovial presence moved quickly across my path. Joe had a way of seeing straight into the soul; he took my hand that moment when I was frozen in place and said softly, "I know who you need to meet."

He introduced me to his friend and my soon-to-be roommate, Kathy, a medical intuitive. That meeting felt less like a coincidence and more like choreography. Through Kathy, I began to trust the subtle again—the tingles, the whispers, the sudden 'knowings'. Each small act of listening rekindled a long-lost friendship with my own intuition.

Around that same time, I discovered Wayne Dyer's audiobooks. One afternoon, he said,
"When you change the way you look at things, the things you look at change." For me, it landed differently: "When you change the way you look at things, the way you look at things changes."

It was all about perception.

That idea rewired my life. I realized awareness had never left; it had only been waiting for me to look again—with curiosity instead of judgment, with wonder instead of fear.

The more I practiced that shift, the clearer the world became. I began each morning by setting an intention, not as a wish, rather as a way of being.

I pictured a simple vase before me. The vase was my overarching intention—peace, freedom, ease. The water inside represented possibility: presence, openness, tranquility. And the flowers I placed within were the expressions of that energy—changing each day, sometimes vibrant, sometimes wilting, and always rooted in the same stillness.

When I saw life that way, nothing felt wasted. Even what seemed to be falling apart was simply returning to feed new growth. And somewhere deep inside, a whisper returned:

What can I build with this?

Integration

Awareness didn't arrive all at once. It returned in fragments—through a breath, a sign, a quiet nudge that said, "Pay attention here."

Every time I chose to listen instead of ignore, and respond instead of react, the world opened a little wider. Choice, I learned, is the most powerful form of prayer.

Each choice reshapes our energy. Awareness doesn't demand we do more; it invites us to be more—present, receptive, aligned. From that alignment, right actions flow naturally, like breath following heartbeat.

Over time, I discovered that intuition isn't a flash of lightning; it's the steady rhythm of the soul breathing through everyday life.

Joe and I stayed friends for years. He became one of those rare souls who show up as both teacher and mirror. From him, I learned how to create labyrinths—sacred pathways that mimic life's spiral.

I told him I wanted to create a horse-led labyrinth, and we'd talk for hours about design, direction, and intention. I remember tracing lines in the dirt, hearing him describe how a labyrinth isn't about reaching the center; it's about the journey inward.

Before the project was finished, Joe passed away. I felt the ache of his absence and the echo of his wisdom. When I finally completed the walking horse labyrinth, I stepped back to admire it, tears and gratitude mingling in my chest.

Then a shadow crossed above me. A hawk—my spirit animal—landed on a post overlooking the labyrinth. It paused, eyes steady, then lifted and glided across to the post on the opposite side before turning back toward me.

In that instant, I knew: it was Joe, offering approval, his spirit reminding me that connection never ends.

That moment anchored everything I had been learning. Awareness, perception, intuition, love—they're all the same current flowing through different names. We lose our way only when we forget to listen.

The more I practiced, the more I noticed that this current connects us all. My own awakening wasn't just personal—it reminded me that when one of us listens deeply, others around us begin to hear their own hearts more clearly, too.

The labyrinth taught me that every turn, even the ones that seem to lead backward, is part of the path home.

Now my days begin with stillness. I sit with my breath, place my hand over my heart, and ask: What is my intention today? Not what do I want to achieve, rather, how do I choose to 'be'?

Some days, the answer is calm. Other days, it's courage, compassion, or curiosity. Whatever arises, I write it down, share it with a friend, breathe it in, and carry it like a quiet song through the day.

Awareness, I've learned, is a living practice—a gentle returning, again and again, to the present moment. Awakening also asks for courage—the courage to stay open even when it's uncomfortable. Those moments of discomfort are sacred stretching; they expand our capacity to hold light.

The awakening within isn't a single event. It's a lifelong conversation with the Divine, disguised as your own voice.

Spiral Steps

- **Pause and Listen** – Take three conscious breaths. Notice what your body is telling you before your mind speaks.
- **Set an Intention** – Each morning, name one quality you wish to embody. Imagine it as the vase that will hold your day.
- **Perception Check** – When challenges arise, ask, "How else could I look at this?" Shifting perception shifts reality.
- **Journal the Whispers** – Record moments of intuition, synchronicity, or grace. Over time, you'll see the pattern of your own spiral.
- **Honor the Signs** – Whether a hawk in the sky or a stranger's kind word, let the world's small messages remind you: you are never alone.
- **Choose Your Response** – Before reacting, pause and ask, "What would love do here?" Each conscious choice becomes an upward turn in your spiral.

Closing Reflection

Every awakening begins with a whisper—an invitation to listen again. Each time we quiet the noise and return to our inner knowing, we plant a seed of trust.

And so I ask, as you pause here:

What can you build with your own awakening?

Because every moment you choose awareness over avoidance, you are already Spiraling Up.

It begins within—not in the striving or the fixing, rather in the remembering. The journey of awakening is a return to being. And from that being, the doing, the creating, and the miracles all naturally unfold.

CHAPTER 2

The Tone of A Whisper

"Sometimes, it takes a storm to show you what's been breaking all along." — **Karen Rudolf**

The Breaking Point

For years, life was measured in school drop-offs, carpools, after-school activities, grocery lists, and a calendar that never left room for me.

I was running six hours a day between three schools, balancing lessons, lunches, and laundry. My own breath had become something I gave away to everyone else.

My former husband meant well. All the same, our lives had grown into parallel lines. When he was home from work, our conversations hovered barely on the surface—bills, schedules, responsibilities. Love had been replaced by logistics.

One Wednesday morning, after another blur of errands, he complained that the house was a mess and that I was not spending enough time with the horses, since they were living beings that needed care.

I heard my own voice rise—sharper than I meant—

> "If I don't take some time to regroup,
> this whole thing falls apart."

The words startled both of us. It wasn't anger; it was truth fighting for air.

So I claimed Wednesday mornings. I'd drop the girls at school, drive straight to the beach, and power-walk until the noise inside me quieted. I'd have lunch by the water and feed the pigeons with my friends, Bill and Betty—a ritual of simple joy that reminded me I was still a person beneath the titles of wife and mother. By the time I picked up the girls that afternoon, I could breathe again.

It wasn't self-indulgence; it was survival. Those Wednesdays became my silent rebellion—one small act of choosing me before the storms began.

Sometimes the smallest choices are the first acts of self-responsibility. *Being* births the right doing; one moment of presence births an entire path of alignment.

Awareness doesn't arrive with a shout; it begins as a whisper asking, *What do you need to breathe again?*

And so, the first thread of awakening began to weave itself quietly into my days. Even then, I didn't realize I was already asking:

What can I build with this *small moment of space?*

Micro-Acts of Self-Recovery

Neuroscience shows that even brief rituals of self-connection—five minutes of breathwork, a walk, a moment of pause—shift the nervous system from survival mode to regulation. Tiny acts of self-honoring become the first steps toward major life realignment.

Peace Before the Storm

The barn was my second sanctuary. The smell of hay and leather, the warmth of Scamper's breath—those were the places where I could hear myself think.

He was my confidant, my steady heartbeat in motion. I'd pour my worries into the air between us, and he'd rest his head on my shoulder as if to say, *I've got you.* I'd lean my forehead against his neck and feel his calm travel through me like medicine. When words failed at home, I found peace in the rhythm of brushing his coat and the quiet trust in his eyes.

Storms don't always announce themselves.

That summer afternoon carried the faint metallic scent of rain before the first drop fell. The sky grumbled, low and distant. I was tightening my daughter's bathing-suit strap when thunder cracked so loud it shook the windows.

I instantly stood up.
I froze.
My heart sank before the phone even rang.
A knowing...
Lightning.
Scamper was gone.

The grief was tidal. My daughters saw me cry for the first time. I tried to stay strong for them. Inside, I was collapsing. I buried the need for meaning, told myself storms were just weather.

Signs? I didn't believe in them yet. I only knew how to keep moving through pain.

Sometimes the first strike doesn't destroy; it awakens. Lightning only reveals what's already waiting in the dark.

Trauma became the first teacher—proof that pain, when faced, can be transformed into purpose. Healing begins the moment we stop resisting the lesson and choose to see meaning within the chaos.

Even as I wept, something inside whispered:
What can I build with this *heartbreak?*

I didn't yet have the answer—and the question had been planted.

Trauma as Catalyst

Trauma collapses old neural pathways and forces the brain into rapid rewiring. When approached consciously, this disruption becomes an opening—an accelerated window for transformation, meaning-making, and identity shift.

The Crack Through the Heart

Grief rearranged the furniture of my soul. I clung to routine—school runs, chores, conversations that skimmed over what was really happening. My marriage unraveled in slow motion until even silence between us felt heavy.

I remember our anniversary that year. We went to dinner, trying too hard to act normal. The conversation turned brittle and small. When we came home, the girls had lit the house with candles and cupcakes.

"Happy Anniversary!" they shouted with glee.

We smiled for their sake, the flickering light making the distance between us even clearer.

The next morning, our nine-year-old asked,

> "Mom, why are you still with Dad? You don't belong together."

Her words hit harder than any argument.

Children see what we try so hard to hide.

That Wednesday, I walked the beach, praying for clarity.

> "Please, God, give me a sign. Make my family whole. Tell me what to do."

And the waves only whispered back:

> *'You already know.'*

One morning at the barn, shoveling manure, I muttered into the dust,

> "I'm too scared to ask for a divorce. The only way out is if he has an affair."

The air went still after I said it.

Be careful what you ask for.

Words hold frequency. Spoken from fear, they build walls; spoken from love, they open doors.

Weeks later, I fell to my knees, exhausted, pleading,

> "Spirit, please—fix my marriage."

That night I dreamed of a tall wooden door floating in the dark. A voice said, *Go in.*

I stepped through. The door slammed behind me, and I fell—down, down—until I stopped fighting and trusted I'd land on my feet.

When I woke, the dream clung to me like morning mist.

It wasn't the rescue I needed; it was surrender. The sacred balance between being and doing began here, trusting the unseen instead of forcing the outcome.

Sometimes, faith means letting go before we see the ground beneath us. And still, deep within me, the same quiet invitation:

What can I build with this ending?

The Energetics of Words

In quantum linguistics, intention amplifies the vibration of spoken words.
Fear-based language narrows possibilities.
Truth-based language expands it.
Your whispered words had already begun shaping the path before you consciously walked it.

Freedom

The divorce lasted three years. Silence became its own language.

When the final papers were signed in 2007, I left the courthouse numb and drove straight to the feed store for hay—because that's what life does; it keeps going.

Backing the truck up to the dock, I felt a sharp jolt—a flat tire. Annoyed, I jumped out, found the culprit—a bent license plate—and tossed it into the truck bed. After AAA fixed the tire and I returned to the barn, I began clearing the truck. The plate caught my eye.

I flipped it over.

F R E E D O M.

I froze, breath caught somewhere between laughter and tears.

A piece of metal from the road had just spoken the word my soul had been craving.

Coincidence? I didn't think so anymore.

That day marked the beginning of my belief that Spirit speaks through signs.

I began noticing them everywhere—songs, feathers, numbers, clouds.

The world was alive with meaning; I just hadn't been listening.

The universe whispers until it must roar. Learn the whisper's tone before the storm returns.

Freedom, I came to learn, isn't about escape—it's about **alignment.** It's the quiet power of choosing your truth, even when it shakes your world apart. Alignment is the language of abundance; when we live in integrity with our soul, the universe reorganizes around that vibration.

The moment we take responsibility for that choice, the spiral turns upward.

And again, I asked:

What can I build with this new beginning?

Why Signs Appear After Major Shifts

When we experience emotional or spiritual rupture, the brain becomes more perceptive to patterns and meaning.

This heightened awareness—paired with intuitive attunement—allows synchronicities to be recognized as guidance rather than randomness.

Spiral Steps

- **Pause for Breath** – Even a single sacred ritual—a weekly walk, five quiet minutes—can reconnect you to yourself.
- **Listen Beneath the Noise** – What truth is your soul whispering that your schedule is drowning out?
- **Speak Carefully** – Words are frequency, shaping the road ahead.
- **Ask for Signs** – Then stay open enough to see them in the ordinary.
- **Redefine Freedom** – It's not escape; it's alignment with truth.
- **Remember** – Every storm reveals a choice: to crumble or to rise.

Choose to **Spiral Up.**

Closing Reflection

Many storms begin as whispers ignored.

Sometimes lightning strikes not to destroy; instead, it illuminates what's been unseen.

Trauma can break us open or break us down—the choice is in the meaning we make of it.

The pain that cracks you apart also hands you the blueprint for rebuilding.

So, as you breathe here at the end of this chapter, ask yourself: ***What can I build with this storm?***

Because the truth is, every crack of thunder carries one quiet invitation: to trust divine timing, surrender the old form, and rise—rebuilt, radiant, and free.

This is how we Spiral UP.

CHAPTER 3

Music for the Soul

"Wherever you are, be there." — **Jim Rohn**

The Background Noise

I grew up in a home where the soundtrack was self-doubting. My mother—loving, loyal, endlessly giving—lived to please others. Her refrain was quiet and constant: *I'm sorry. I'm not enough. I'll try harder next time.*

When you're a child, you don't question the melody; you learn the tune. So, I grew up believing that self-sacrifice equaled love, that worth had to be earned, and that silence was safer than song.

For years, I carried that frequency inside me—the low hum of *not enough.* It became the rhythm beneath my thoughts, shaping every choice and every relationship until I could no longer tell where her voice ended, and mine began.

Eventually, the ache to find something more sent me searching outside myself. I studied world quantum physics, neuroscience, religions, philosophies—anything that promised light.

I was looking for proof of worth, of love, of God—somewhere *out there*—never realizing it had been within me all along.

We inherit not only stories, also soundtracks. Trauma writes its melody in our nervous system until we learn to rewrite the score. What once hummed as fear can, with awareness, become faith.

Inherited Soundtracks

We don't just inherit eye color and mannerisms—we also absorb emotional "music": tone, language, and belief patterns. These become subconscious loops in the nervous system. The good news? With awareness, we can re-tune them. What was once a fear frequency can be rewritten into a song of self-worth.

Finding Faith in Frequency

The turning point came in Orlando, when my boyfriend took me to a huge church called Northland. Seven hundred plus people filled the sanctuary. The lights dimmed, guitars began to strum, drums rolled—and then a wall of sound rose around me.

And it was the sermon that moved me. Even more was the music.

Upbeat praise songs—pop, joyful, alive—echoed through the room with lyrics like *I am enough. God loves me. Trust yourself.* I sang so loudly the first time that I startled myself. I was crying and smiling all at once. The vibration rolled through my chest like a heartbeat I had forgotten belonged to me.

After the service, I asked Pastor Joel Hunter, who's since retired—a kind man who would become a mentor—why people came every Sunday, dressed in their finest, sang their hearts out, and then went home unchanged.

He smiled gently.

"Karen," he said, "that's why you and I are here—to be messengers and create change."

That sentence became a new chord in my life: I wasn't here just to heal; I was here to *resonate.*

The moment I chose to embody that message, a new frequency began to rise within me—one built not on proving my worth but on living it. 'Being' became the instrument; doing became the echo.

And quietly, the question returned:
What can I build with this harmony I've found?

Why Music Hits the Heart First

Group singing and music activate brain regions tied to emotion, connection, and reward. They release dopamine and oxytocin—the "feel-good" and "bonding" chemicals—that support us in feeling safe enough to open up. That's why lyrics like *I am enough* don't just land as words; they land as embodied truth.

The Language of Energy

Music had always been part of me—classical records from my father's collection, jazz spinning on lazy Sundays, musical theater echoing through the house, and the less-than-sacred fif and bugle corps that blasted us awake every weekend.

Later came Yanni concerts that left me in tears, and the countless times I danced around the kitchen just to feel emotion move through my body.

That's the thing about music—it moves energy, shifting one's psychological state.

And energy *is* life.

I came to see that everything is vibration. Our thoughts, our words, our bodies—they're all instruments. When energy flows freely, we experience harmony. When we attempt to hold everything perfectly still, we call it balance.

That kind of balance is motionless—it stops the dance. Harmony is movement. Balance is stillness.

Healing happens when we allow energy to flow. When I stopped *trying* to stay "balanced" and started to live in harmony, my whole world softened. It wasn't about holding everything in control anymore; it was about learning to sway with life.

In that sway, I discovered alignment—the true currency of success. When our inner tone matches our intention, life orchestrates the rest through divine timing. No forcing, no pushing—just the natural rhythm of resonance.

Harmony vs. Balance

"Perfect balance" often keeps us rigid, braced, and over-controlled. Harmony, on the other hand, is dynamic—like an orchestra constantly adjusting, listening, and flowing. The nervous system thrives on *healthy* movement and variation, not frozen stillness.

The Rhythm of Creation

As my spiritual practice deepened, I began each morning with soft piano music, coffee, and my journal. I wrote three words to define my intention for the day—peace, grace, courage—and ended each night reflecting on what those words had taught me.

The simple rhythm of morning and evening journaling became a song of its own. Over time, patterns began to appear—threads of thought that wove into insight.

One morning, as the music played in the background, I looked down at the page and saw a mosaic forming—thoughts connecting in colors and shapes rather than lines and lists.

That moment birthed what would become Thread~Z, Connections to our inner thoughts, and the precursor to Tranquil SOULutions Mind Mosaic™ Clarity Tool.

Music was always playing while I created—soft piano, ambient tones—frequencies that quieted the thinking mind and opened the intuitive one.

I took the work globally, leading sessions at creativity conferences where people pulled cards and discovered that clarity was not something they found, rather something they *felt.*

Each refinement, each new insight, came with a soundtrack. Music turned confusion into flow, noise into knowing.

Every note asked the same question:
What can I build with this sound*, this silence, this moment of inspiration?*

Creation, I learned, is collaboration with Spirit—the dance between surrender and action, stillness and movement, being and doing. When we listen inwardly first, the right outward action follows effortlessly.

Creativity, Music, and the Brain

Gentle, rhythmic music can shift the brain from high-beta "overthinking" into more relaxed alpha and theta states—the same states associated with creativity, intuition, and insight.

This is how my Mind Mosaic and books appeared when the music was playing; my mind had dropped from analyzing into *allowing*.

The Dance of Connection

Today, music fills my home again—sometimes soft instrumentals while I write, sometimes the joyful chaos of dancing in the kitchen while I cook or clean.

My daughters and I once took Suzuki lessons together: violin for them, later, piano for us all. They'd nudge me off the bench mid-practice, giggling, their tiny fingers finding the notes faster than mine.

It was the purest expression of harmony—different hands, same song.

Now, I use music with my clients—during meditations, breathwork, and visualizations—because vibration opens the heart faster than logic ever could.

When the rhythm steadies, the nervous system remembers safety. When we hum, chant, or breathe in sync, energy begins to flow again.

Heart-focused breathing, a practice I later studied through HeartMath as a practitioner, taught me that when we recall gratitude or appreciation, the heart and brain fall into coherence. In that coherence, fear dissolves. We can't hold fear and gratitude in the same heartbeat.

I recall a time I was practicing with my dog and our horse Truman, as I watched their chests rise and fall, my breath would sync with theirs. When Truman was anxious, I'd control my breath, and he'd calm down and breathe in sync with me. I was fascinated. **What can I build with this?**

Harmony isn't about perfection; it's about connection. When one person re-tunes to peace, everyone nearby feels the shift. When we each find our own rhythm, the world begins to hum in tune.

Heart Coherence in Real Life

HeartMath research shows that when we focus on gratitude or appreciation, the heart's rhythm becomes smooth and ordered. This "coherence" influences brain function and even those around us—humans and animals alike. Calming my breath literally became a tuning fork for Truman's nervous system.

Trusting the Rhythm

Riding, like music, taught my daughters—and me—how to trust the rhythm of life.

When they were little, I'd tell them,

"Close your eyes, hold on, trust the movement of the horse. Feel the rhythm."

It wasn't just about balance in the saddle; it was about surrender. It was learning that flow has its own intelligence—and that harmony comes when we stop fighting the motion and begin to move with it.

Today, they all love to dance. Their bodies remember what their souls learned on horseback—that rhythm is trust in motion. That energy, when trusted, carries us exactly where we're meant to go.

And still, the question remains:
What can I build with this rhythm that carries me?

Spiral Steps

- **Morning Intention** – Begin each day with three words that describe how you want to *feel.* Let them become your inner rhythm.
- **Evening Reflection** – Journal what those words taught you. Notice where harmony appeared and where resistance asked to be softened.
- **Sound Reset** – Play a piece of music that matches your mood. Let your breath move with the beat for three minutes; feel your energy re-tune.
- **Energy Awareness** – Ask *Where am I flowing, and where am I frozen?* Use breath, sound, or gentle movement to restore coherence.
- **Stillness Practice** – Sit in silence long enough to hear your heartbeat. That's your soul keeping time with the Divine.

Closing Reflection

Music is the conversation between the Spirit and the nervous system. When we listen—*truly listen*—we hear our own heartbeat syncing with the universe.

Each rhythm, each silence, each song invites one simple question: ***What can I build with this harmony?***

Because every note—joyful or aching—adds to the symphony of our becoming. As we learn to trust the rhythm, we don't just find peace— We remember that we *are* the music.

CHAPTER 4

The Word As Wand — Speaking Life Into Being

"In the beginning was the Word..." — **John 1:1**

Sound is the first act of creation.

Before there was light, there was vibration—a pulse that carried every thought, whisper, and breath. We continued that original frequency. Words are not only how we describe the world; they are how we design it.

For most of my life, I didn't realize I'd been creating with my words all along. I used them the way most people do—to fill silence, to explain, to defend, to pray—never sensing the architecture I was building beneath each sentence.

Only later did I learn that *abracadabra*—the magician's incantation of wonder—comes from the Aramaic for ***"I create as I speak."*** We are all magicians in this way, whether we know it or not.

Sound Before Light

Ancient wisdom and modern physics agree on something profound: everything is vibration. Sound is structured vibration. When we speak, we're not just making noise—we're sending organized waves into a responsive field.

Your words are not passive; they are *creative frequencies*.

Be Careful What You Ask For

I remember standing in the barn, straw sticking to my boots, the smell of rain in the air. I was exhausted from trying to hold together a marriage that had already begun to fray. I whispered into the dust, *"I don't have the strength to ask for a divorce. The only way out is if he has an affair."*

It wasn't a proclamation—it was a plea from a woman on her knees, half prayer, half surrender.

And the universe, obedient and neutral, answered exactly as spoken.

That moment became my initiation into the power of words. Every thought and sentence is a seed cast into the fertile soil of energy. Some sprout into blessings, others into lessons, and all eventually take form.

The tongue can plant roses or thorns; the ground doesn't judge—it simply grows what it's given.

It took me years to understand that this wasn't about guilt or punishment; it was about resonance. Energy amplifies whatever we feed it. When our speech vibrates with fear, life mirrors that frequency. When we speak from faith, life harmonizes in return.

Our words are instructions to the universe, and the universe— faithful and impartial—obeys.

That night in the barn taught me one of life's hardest lessons: Be careful what you ask for—and more importantly, be aware of *how* you ask. And later, when I was ready, the whisper returned: *What can I build with this awareness?*

The Barn & the Feedback Loop

What we speak repeatedly becomes what we expect.

What we expect shapes what we notice.

What we notice informs what we choose.

And what we choose reinforces what we speak.

This is the loop of creation—words are often the first domino.

The Frequency of Belief

Words without belief are hollow. I can stand before a mirror and declare, *"I am brilliant,"* yet if my body flinches and my mind whispers *"liar,"* nothing changes. Energy follows alignment, not grammar.

That's why I teach *mind-shift*, not *mindset*. A *set* is fixed, like concrete. A *shift* is movement—like breath, like rhythm, like grace.

When belief rises to meet the word, frequency coheres. It's like tuning a radio—you can't hear joy on the station of doubt. Change the frequency, and the song changes.

Speak what you desire to feel, not what you fear will happen. Your words are your wand. Use them with awareness. *Being* births the right 'doing'; vibration births the right result.

So I ask again, What might I build with this knowledge?

Belief + Word = Coherence

Affirmations don't work because we say them; they work when our bodies begin to *believe* them. The shift happens when we move from "performing" words to *embodying* them—when our breath, posture, and intention line up with what we're saying.

The Power and Consequence of Words

I once witnessed how a few frustrated words spoken to a child carved deep grooves in her confidence. Children believe what they hear about themselves until they learn to rewrite that narrative. We all do.

I learned that again when one of my daughters said during my transformation, *"Mom, I want my old mom back."*

Without thinking, I replied, "That mom has died; this is who I am now."

The words landed like stones. I hadn't meant to wound—I simply didn't yet know how to translate my awakening into tenderness.

Later, through tears, I realized how language can either build bridges or burn them. Awareness turns the same words into healing tools. When spoken from truth, language resurrects connection. Each sentence we speak either moves us closer to or further from love.

The key is listening to the echo—what our words leave behind in the hearts of others. Vulnerability is not weakness; it's the amplifier that lets love be heard.

The Echo of a Sentence

Our nervous systems remember *tone* and *impact* long after they forget the exact words.

This is why a single sentence can replay for decades, shaping how safe—or unsafe—we feel being ourselves.

The Word as Medicine — How the Body Listens

Every cell is tuned to the language of the mind. When we say *"I'm exhausted,"* the body complies. When we whisper *"I am safe,"* the nervous system exhales. The body eavesdrops on every conversation we have with ourselves.

During my accident in Costa Rica, I was told my chances of walking were slim to none. Long before medicine caught up, I spoke to my body with gratitude and vision—imagining light moving through my joints.

"Every day, in every way, my body is healing on a cellular level. Thank you, thank you, thank you." I spoke like a broken record.

Little by little, the pain softened. My words became medicine; my body began to heal. Science now affirms what mystics have always known: sound alters cell resonance.

When gratitude and breath join speech, heart-brain coherence restores flow. We cannot hold fear and appreciation in the same heartbeat. The body, like the universe, listens with love.

Cells That Hear You

Emerging fields like psychoneuroimmunology show that thoughts and emotions influence immune response, inflammation, and healing. When you pair intentional words with breath and genuine feeling, you're not "faking it"—you're giving your body a new script to follow.

The Ripple of Expectation

Expectation can disguise itself as hope, and it often carries the weight of control. It narrows energy into a single outcome and stops the natural flow of receiving.

As a little girl, my babysitter was the television. I grew up watching *Father Knows Best* and other shows where every husband was tender, every father patient, and every conflict resolved neatly by the end of the episode. Those scenes became my silent blueprint for how life should look.

When I married, I projected that script onto my former husband—expecting him to be the ever-present, endlessly affectionate father I'd seen on-screen. He, of course, had his own history, his own unspoken wounds, and did the best he could with what life had taught him. My disappointment wasn't really in him; it was in the picture I was comparing him to.

Expectation became a dam in the river of our relationship. **Flow requires allowance, not demand.**

When I finally released the story of how love *should* look, I began to see the love that was already there. During the years after my divorce, I often told my daughters,

"Your father loves you the best he can with what he has."

Each time I spoke those words, they softened something in me, too. That sentence became a bridge built from compassion—proof that gentle language can heal generations in both directions.

Words ripple forward and backward through time. When we speak forgiveness, we untie the knots that bind both the past and the future. Forgiveness, compassion, and gratitude—they're all frequencies of freedom.

Words Across Generations

What we say about others—especially parents—becomes part of the emotional DNA our children carry as their inner script. Speaking compassion over someone's limitations doesn't excuse harm; rather, it stops the inheritance of bitterness. Compassionate language can also protect them from carrying resentment that doesn't belong to them. Gentle language heals generations

Seeing Through a New Lens

Years later, I was reminded of that truth through another mirror of love. Someone close to me—brilliant, creative, and wired to see the world through a kaleidoscope of possibilities—lived in what often looked like chaos to my structured mind. Whenever I visited, I found myself tightening inside, trying to "fix" what didn't match my version of calm.

One afternoon over lunch, something beautiful happened. They were speaking with a friend who shared their same rhythm—two bright minds leaping joyfully from thought to thought, finishing each other's sentences, weaving laughter between bursts of insight.

I watched, listening more than speaking, and suddenly the scene shifted. The energy that once made me uneasy now shimmered with genius and connection. They weren't scattered; they were symphonic—playing music I hadn't learned to hear.

It struck me like a soft awakening: **it wasn't them who needed to change—it was my lens.**

I had been looking through inherited filters, those old *Father Knows Best* ideals that equated neatness with worthiness and order with love. I had mistaken difference for disorder, individuality for imbalance.

The moment I saw through that illusion, judgment dissolved. I understood that every soul has its own way of organizing life, its own divine rhythm. What looks like chaos may simply be creativity expressing itself without permission. What feels unfamiliar might just be brilliance moving in a pattern only Spirit understands.

I realized love isn't about aligning someone to our measure of comfort—it's about expanding enough to meet them where they are. **Acceptance became my new form of prayer.** That day, I exhaled years of expectation.

I stopped trying to make life fit inside my picture frame and began admiring the art exactly as it was painted. In that release, something holy unfolded: peace.

Sometimes spiraling up doesn't mean changing what's before you— it means widening your heart until everything, and everyone finds its rightful place in love.

Speaking As Creation

Before we can speak light into others, we must learn to speak it into ourselves. The voice that narrates your life becomes the architect of your reality. Each word you speak is either a brick or a bridge.

My daily practice is simple:

- **Word Audit:** Notice the phrases that escape your mouth. Do they shrink or expand you?
- **Cancel / Delete / Reframe:** When a limiting phrase appears, whisper *Cancel.* Replace it with truth.
- **HeartSpeak:** Hand on heart, breathe slowly, and speak one word you wish to embody today—*Peace. Flow. Enough.*
- **Journal:** Write what you wish to grow. Each word is a seed.

Language becomes light when belief and breath unite.
What you speak over yourself becomes the reality you walk through.

So ask: ***What can I build with the words I choose today?***

Spiral Steps — Speaking as Creation

- **Listen Within:** For one day, track your inner dialogue like background music. What's the tone?
- **Pause Before Responding:** Let intention meet breath before words meet air.
- **Reframe:** Transform one habitual phrase into something that expands possibility.
- **Affirm Aloud:** "I am the author of my words, and they are creating my world."
- **Observe:** Watch how reality begins to echo back the words you choose.

Closing Reflection

Every word is a vibration that builds or breaks the bridge between where you are and who you're becoming. Speech is the first tool of transformation—each sentence a seed, each whisper a spell.

So the question returns, soft but certain:

What can I build with this word?

Because when we learn to speak life into being, we don't just change our world—we change the frequency of everyone who hears us.

"Every word is a spell, every sentence a seed.
Speak love, and the universe will learn your
language." — **Karen Rudolf**

CHAPTER 5

Value & Flow:
The Currency of Self-Worth

"When I began valuing myself, life finally mirrored it back." — **Karen Rudolf**

The Inheritance of Lack

My mother used to save the ends of things—rubber bands, stray buttons, worn plugs from old toasters. She'd drop them into a drawer that smelled faintly of metal and dust, a small graveyard of forgotten *maybes.*

"Never throw anything away," she'd say. "You never know when you'll need it."

As a child, I didn't see a woman being resourceful; I saw a woman afraid there wouldn't be enough. That drawer became my first classroom in scarcity. I learned that you saved the good dishes for guests, the good shoes for Sundays, and the good dreams for *someday.*

Even love had to be rationed carefully—measured, earned, and rarely overflowing. Being the middle child, I wore my sister's hand-medowns—clothes that carried her scent and story. They fit awkwardly, like someone else's skin. It wasn't just fabric; it was a message: *you get what's left.*

Looking back, I know now, as a single mother, that my mother meant well. She was doing her best inside the belief system she inherited. And what I absorbed wasn't her thrift—it was her fear.

I learned that money was tied to worth, and worth was always slightly out of reach.

For years, I lived from that drawer—emotionally and spiritually. I gave away my energy freely, over-delivered, under-charged, and apologized for having needs. I became fluent in self-sacrifice, believing that love required exhaustion and that success demanded struggle.

And yet, beneath the noise, a whisper persisted: *There's more than this.* The spiral was calling.

And soon, the river would answer.

The Legacy of Scarcity

Scarcity is not a personality trait; it's an inherited nervous-system imprint.

Children absorb the emotional economy of their home:
— how money is talked about
— how needs are handled
— how worth is expressed

Scarcity becomes a *frequency*, not a fact — until we choose a different song.

The River and Harriet the Blue Heron

After my divorce, I moved to a small home on the river—a place where silence spoke louder than words. Each morning, I'd sit on the weathered dock, coffee steaming beside me, crumbling bits of bread into the ripples.

The water shifted like glass kissed by breath. Fish rose in flashes of silver. It felt like communion—me, the river, and the hum of life itself.

Every morning, *Harriet* came—a tall, elegant blue heron with feathers the color of stormlight.

She'd perch on the fallen log beside me, still and regal. Then, in one effortless motion, she'd strike the water and surface with a fish.

Again and again, she'd dive—and yet, the river never emptied.

That moment re-wrote my definition of wealth. Abundance wasn't about having; it was about trusting the flow. Nature didn't hoard or question. It simply received and released.

As I watched Harriet, I began whispering affirmations not about wealth, rather about worth:

> "I am supported."
> "I am part of the flow."
> "There is always more where that came from."

Then came the question that now lives in all my work:
What can I build with this?

The answer was clear: a new story of enoughness.

Nature's Prosperity Model

Nature never operates from scarcity.

Rivers replenish. Trees regrow. Seasons cycle.

Abundance is not accumulation — it's circulation.

True wealth is **receiving without fear** and **giving without depletion.**

Permission to Receive

For years, I drove my faithful old Tahoe—the car that carried soccer gear, horse saddles, and the heartbeat of family life. It was practical, reliable... and joyless. Deep inside, I longed for something that symbolized *freedom,* not duty.

As a young girl, I'd trail my father through car shows, tracing the curves of an SL 500 convertible with my eyes, whispering, *Someday.*

After my divorce, "someday" still felt far away—until a friend said, "Karen, it doesn't have to be new." That single phrase cracked something open.... Permission.

Soon after, I found her: a sleek black SL 500 with soft leather seats that felt like home and horizon all at once. When I slid behind the wheel, the engine purred, the top lowered, and the wind tangled through my hair. I laughed—a deep, full-bodied laugh that came from the place where aliveness resides..

I wasn't buying a car; I was reclaiming my permission to receive. It wasn't about the price tag; it was about alignment with joy.

Abundance doesn't wait for worthiness; it responds to openness. The more I appreciated that car, the more life mirrored it back in unexpected ways—clients, opportunities, friends. Joy is magnetic.

And again I asked, ***What can I build with this?***
The answer: **Possibility.**

Receiving as a Skill

Receiving is an act of nervous-system expansion.

If we grew up equating self-worth with self-sacrifice, receiving feels unsafe.

But joy calibrates the body to *allow* more — without guilt.

Lessons in Loss and Stewardship

Then came the next lesson: *stewardship.*

I invested in a wellness retreat with someone who promised partnership and profit. The event ended—and so did the promises. Not long after, another smooth talker appeared—a coach from overseas offering visions of expansion and love. I trusted. I sent money. He vanished.

At first, shame consumed me. I felt foolish and betrayed. And when I stopped resisting the pain, I realized: I hadn't just lost money— I had paid *tuition to the universe.*

I had purchased discernment. I had bought back the right to trust myself.

When I released the anger, gratitude entered. I still had a home. My children were safe. The river still shimmered outside my window.

So again, I asked, ***What can I build with this?*** And the answer rose softly: **Wisdom.**

Since then, I've never invested from desperation—only from alignment. When I give now, it's from fullness, not fear. Because trauma, when transformed, becomes the fuel for purpose.

The Cost of Intuition

Intuition becomes stronger each time we *survive* ignoring it.

Pain becomes tuition.

Discernment becomes the diploma.

The Energetics of Value

Value is not a number; it's a vibration. Money is simply the mirror that makes vibration visible. When we treat money as energy in motion, we see its sacred nature. It wants to circulate—like breath, like tide, like love.

Holding too tightly creates stagnation. Giving without boundaries drains the current.

But giving and receiving in harmony? That's *flow.*

Balance is static—it demands control. Harmony is alive—it invites trust.

For years, I spent unconsciously—on guilt, on fear, on proving my worth. Each time I said *yes* when I meant *no,* I wrote an energetic check I couldn't cash. Each time I undercharged, I declared, *I am worth less.* Each time I over-gave, I whispered, *You matter more than I do.*

And when I began valuing my time, peace, and presence, my outer world shifted.

Clients began paying joyfully. Money arrived through channels I hadn't imagined.

Generosity no longer depleted me—it replenished me.

Generosity, when aligned, is a declaration of trust.

Even scripture reminds us: "In the beginning was the Word." Sound became form.

Energy became matter.

Our internal dialogue is the currency that writes our reality. When I speak abundance, I attune to creation. When I speak scarcity, I contract from it. The choice is always mine.

So I ask once more: **What can I build with this?**
The answer: *Harmony.*

Value as Vibration

Your prices don't reflect your worth —
they reflect your energetic boundaries.
When you value your presence, time, and peace,
the world simply rises to meet the frequency you set.

Spiral Steps — Re-Tuning to Flow

- **Flow Inventory** – Where is abundance already present yet unnoticed—in laughter, breath, sunlight, time?
- **Permission to Receive** – Hand over heart, whisper: *I am open. I am worthy. I allow.*
- **Energy Audit** – List where energy leaks—overgiving, guilt, unaligned commitments—and release them.
- **Worth Ledger** – Record three ways you added value today: through presence, kindness, or creation.
- **Seed Question** – End your day asking, *What can I build with this?* and let silence answer.

Closing Reflection

Abundance isn't measured by possessions; it's revealed through peace. Value doesn't come from what we earn; it's born from how we honor what we have. Flow isn't something to chase—it's something to trust.

When I finally began valuing myself, life didn't give me *more things*—it gave me *more meaning*.

It reflected back the worth I had always carried within. We spiral UP when we circulate love, gratitude, and generosity with grace. We spiral UP when we build bridges instead of walls.

We spiral UP when we stop asking *"Do I have enough?"* and start asking,

"What can I build with this?"

"Abundance isn't what we have—it's what we allow." — **Karen Rudolf**

CHAPTER 6

Abracadabra: Words Create Reality

"The declared word is the breath of becoming."
— **Karen Rudolf**

The Breath That Casts The Spell.

We've already covered the power of words. This chapter is about the *craft* of words—**how to use them like a tool.**

Abracadabra isn't a magician's trick—it's a reminder.

From the Aramaic: "I create as I speak."

Not because the world bends to our wishes...rather because **speech is a decision made audible.**

A command given to your nervous system. A direction set for your next choice.

Before a word leaves the mouth, there's a moment most people skip: the inhale.

That inhale is the difference between reacting and creating.

When breath leads, language becomes intentional. When breath is missing, language becomes automatic—old scripts, old defenses, old endings.

So in this chapter, we're not talking about "saying nice things." We're talking about **speaking like you mean it.** Like someone who understands that words are not decoration.

They're designed.

Creation as Vibration

Both ancient texts and modern physics describe reality as vibration. Words are structured vibrations—directing energy into form. You're not "just talking"; you're *tuning* reality.

Breath makes room for intention. Intention gives words direction. Direction turns words into reality—not mystically, but practically— through what you do next, what you tolerate, what you choose, and what you repeat.

So before we go further, we start here:
inhale... then speak.

The Language I Inherited

I was raised in a home filled with love and also with the soft hum of apology. My mother—tender, selfless, endlessly giving—lived inside the frequency of lack.

"I'm sorry."
"I'll try."
"I can't afford to."
"I should have."

Those phrases floated through the air like dust motes—unseen, but everywhere.

As a child, I absorbed their rhythm. When you grow up hearing *I'm not enough*, it becomes a lullaby you no longer question.

I didn't understand that her words were spells and she, like me, was only repeating what had been spoken into her.

Years later, when I began coaching, I challenged her gently: "Mom, every time you say *try*, you owe me a quarter."

She laughed, but she played along. Each *try* cost twenty-five cents.

When the jar was full, she smiled:

"I'm taking my friend to lunch. I always said I couldn't afford it."

She never used '*try*' again. She'd turned trying into doing. The same thing happened with my clients—awareness leads to choice, and choice reshapes reality.

That was the first time I saw someone rewrite reality through language. My mother's speech changed, and so did her life.

I began to wonder—what if the whole world works this way?

Micro-Edits, Macro-Shifts

Replacing one tiny word—like *try*—reteaches the nervous system where power lives.

"I'll try" keeps change out of the future.

"I choose" brings it into the present moment where action happens.

This is the other side of abracadabra—why conscious language matters as much in our lowest moments as it does in our highest.

When Words Become Flesh

If Chapter 4 revealed the power of words, this is where we learn **precision**—so we stop building outcomes we never meant to order.

It stopped being theory for me in a barn as a storm rolled in.

Bone-tired, I whispered into the straw:

"I don't have the strength to ask for a divorce. The only way out is if he has an affair."

It was desperation disguised as surrender. And it taught me something I couldn't unlearn:

words aren't harmless. They're *not* just sound. They're direction.

Not because life is waiting to punish us for a sentence—rather because what we repeatedly speak becomes the story we organize ourselves around. We act in alignment with it. We tolerate it in alignment with it. We make choices that match it.

That day became an initiation:
Words are agreements we make with ourselves—sometimes unconsciously.

Every thought, every whisper, every half-prayer is a seed.

Some plant relief. Some plant thorns. The field doesn't judge. It simply responds to what it's been given.

It took me years to stop blaming myself and start awakening. I wasn't being punished. I was being shown the mechanics of creation— and the responsibility that comes with speaking.

Faith Spoken Aloud

When lightning struck my horse, Truman, and the vet said:

"Put him down—it will cost you a fortune," I took a deep breath and declared:
"He will not only survive—he will thrive, and together, we will become catalysts for change."

That wasn't denial. It was a decision.

That day in Gainesville, the specialist insisted his eye must come out.

As I sat in the butterfly garden, a giant white butterfly landed on my finger.

Looking at it, I whispered: "No. He will see again." They thought I was crazy.

A year later, he was seeing from that same eye.

Truman became the living proof of declaration made flesh.

That was the day I stopped *hoping* and started *commanding in love.*

And again, I asked myself:
What can I build with this?

Signs & Declaration

When we declare from love, life often sends physical confirmations—a butterfly, a feather, a timing "coincidence."

These aren't required for creation, rather they encourage the heart to keep believing.

The Word as Medicine — How the Body Listens

We've talked about the power of words. Here's where we make them **usable**—as a daily practice of conscious declaration.

The body doesn't argue with our inner language.
It rehearses it.

"I'm exhausted" becomes a posture.
"I'm safe" becomes a breath.

After my horseback riding accident in Costa Rica—fractures, dislocation, and a surgeon's blunt conclusion—he said,
"just so you're aware, your chances of walking again may be slim to none. I'll do my best."

I took one breath and said, *"Watch me."*

In that moment, words stopped being commentary and became *commitment.*

I chose a sentence I could live inside:

"Every day, in every way, my body is healing on a cellular level. Thank you, thank you, thank you!" I'd repeat it 3 times, getting more and more commanding each time.

A whisper became a rhythm.
A rhythm became a signal.
A signal became a new normal.

Eight months later, I wasn't just walking. I was living.

This is the holy trinity of creation: what you *believe,* what you *embody,* and what you *speak.*

Sound is the bridge between faith and form.

Declarations are not wishes. They are directional.
And when we speak from love, life sometimes leaves little breadcrumbs—a feather, a butterfly, a perfectly timed message.

Not because we need a sign to be supported...
Rather because the heart loves to be reminded: keep going.

The Body's Secret Language

Your cells respond to emotional tone and mental imagery.

When words, breath, and belief line up, you're not "being unrealistic"—you're giving your biology a new script to follow.

The Science Behind the Spell — Dr. Emoto & The Frequency of Thought**

For as long as I can remember, I believed that every thought affects every cell in the body.

Each cell affects each organ. Every organ reflects ease or disease based on the frequency of our internal world.

When I later studied the work of **Dr. Masaru Emoto**, everything clicked into place.

His research revealed:

- Water exposed to loving words formed beautiful crystalline patterns
- Water exposed to hateful or fearful words became distorted
- Frequency literally shaped form

And because the human body is **70% water**, this truth becomes life-changing:

Our words sculpt our biology.
Our thoughts design our chemistry.
Our emotions instruct our cells.

Dr. Emoto's photographs showed what I'd always sensed:

When we speak love, the body organizes itself around healing. When we speak fear, the body contracts into protection.

Our language doesn't just shape our experiences—*it shapes our physiology.*

Healing is not just a physical process; it is a vibrational one.

You Are Living Water

If water can change structure from a single phrase, imagine what a lifetime of inner dialogue can do.

Every loving word is like pouring fresh, clear water through your entire system.

The Tone Beneath the Words

It isn't only *what* we say—it's how we say it.

Tone carries frequency.
Frequency carries intention.
Intention carries creation.

"I'm fine," spoken through clenched teeth, calls for rescue. "I am safe," spoken with trust, tells the body to relax.

When I understood this, I stopped using words like *help*—they imply brokenness. Instead, I speak of support, partnership, and co-creation.

Every tone is a tuning fork. When we speak in harmony, the world hums back.

Hum, **what can I build with this?**

The Frequency of Fear and Faith

Every word is born from one of two roots: fear or love.

Fear contracts. Love expands.
Fear asks, *What if it doesn't work?*
Love whispers, *What if it does?*

Fear once guided many of my choices—soft, familiar, limiting.

It didn't always shout. Sometimes it whispered, "stay safe," when it truly meant "stay small."

Fear freezes. Faith frees.

When I began creating the Tranquil SOULutions Mind Mosaic™ Clarity Tool, it was born from that freeze—a longing to understand where fear had built walls and how love could dissolve them.

Now I ask myself: Is this coming from fear or from love?

Because the vibration behind our words becomes the architecture of our reality.

The Embodied Practice

Morning:
Hand over heart, whisper one intention—Peace. Flow. Grace.

Day:
Listen for tone. If it feels off, soften. Return to your word.

Evening:
Journal what your words built, shifted, or softened.

Abracadabra is *not* fantasy; it is frequency made visible.

Word Alchemy in Action

The magic isn't in the word—it's in the energy behind it.

To further support you to embody *"I create as I speak"* in daily life, here's a simple reference for raising the vibration of your language.

Each low-frequency phrase keeps energy small; each higher-frequency choice expands it.

Low → High (and why it matters):

- *Try → Choose / Commit / Begin* — "Try" implies doubt; "Choose" affirms power.
- *Should → I intend / I choose to / I get to* — Replaces shame with conscious will.
- *Need / Have to → I am ready to / I desire to / I choose to* — Turns obligation into aligned action.
- *Help me → Support me / Partner with me* — Invites empowerment, not rescue.
- *I can't → I am learning / I am becoming able* — Transforms limitation into growth.
- *Sorry (for existing) → Thank you for understanding / I appreciate your patience* — Shifts guilt into gratitude.
- *Busy → I'm in flow / I'm prioritizing* — Chaos becomes choice.
- *Someday → Now / I'm taking one step today* — Brings the dream into motion.
- *Hard / Impossible → Challenging / Possible with faith* — Reframes resistance as learning.
- *I'm trying to heal → I am healing / I am whole and integrating* — Declares process and completion.

- *I'm fine → I'm feeling / I'm noticing / I'm processing* — Opens honesty and awareness.
- *Problem → Opportunity / Lesson / Invitation* — Directs energy toward creation.
- *Fear → Curiosity / Awareness / Faith* — Fear freezes; curiosity moves.
- *I don't know → I'm open to clarity / The answer will come* — Creates space for intuition.
- *I hope → I trust / I believe / I am creating* — Hope waits; trust acts.
- *I'm stuck → I'm pausing / I'm integrating / I'm realigning* — Honors stillness as sacred recalibration.

Practice:

1. Listen—catch one habitual phrase you use.
2. Breathe—pause before repeating it.
3. Replace—speak its higher-frequency version aloud.
4. Anchor—tap your heart three times as you say it.
5. Notice—the shift isn't subtle; it's cellular.

"If my words are brushstrokes of creation, what masterpiece am I painting today?" ***What can you build and create with this?***

When you speak from love instead of lack, language becomes light. This is how the unseen becomes seen—one conscious word at a time.

Closing Reflection: The Living Word

Sound is the bridge between the unseen and the seen. Each time we speak, we choose which world to strengthen—the one of fear or the one of faith. We are never voiceless; we are always vibrating.

So breathe. Speak softly and with conviction. Your voice is the divine instrument through which life becomes art.

The Water & Word Ritual

Choose a glass of water. Hold it between your palms for ten seconds.

Speak one word into it: Love. Clarity. Strength. Healing.

Drink slowly. Feel it enter your body with intention.

Ask yourself: *"What vibration am I feeding my cells today?"*

This is how thought becomes matter and matter becomes movement.

What can I build with this word?

Spiral Steps – Speak as Creation

- **Audit Your Language:** Are you planting seeds of power or apology?
- **Cancel / Delete / Reframe:** Catch an old pattern midstream and shift it.
- **Tone Practice:** Speak your intention out loud; feel where it lands.
- **Daily Declaration:** Choose one word each morning to embody.
- **Silent Listening:** Hear what the universe whispers back. Creation is a conversation.

"Every breath is a beginning. Every word is a world. Speak love, and watch the universe rearrange itself to listen." — **Karen Rudolf**

CHAPTER 7

Perception & Perspective: Seeing Through New Eyes

"When you change the way you look at things, the way you look at things change." — **Karen Rudolf**

The Lens of Living

Perception and perspective are dance partners—one interprets, the other directs. Perception is what I make something mean; perspective is how I choose to see it.

For years, I took both as unquestioned truth. And truth is rarely fixed—it's filtered. Every moment passes through lenses of experience, emotion, and expectation. Change the lens, and the entire picture transforms.

(A note on a beloved quote: Wayne Dyer said, "When you change the way you look at things, the things you look at change." The version my heart heard was, "When you change the way you look at things, the way you look at things change." That slight shift matters to me; it reminds me that seeing differently is itself a transformation.)

Perception vs. Perspective

Perception is the story your nervous system tells about what's happening.
Perspective is the altitude you choose to view that story from.
Shift either one, and the emotional experience changes—even if the facts don't.

The Bathroom and the Breath

It didn't happen on a mountaintop. It happened in a bathroom. We were circling the same argument again. I followed him, words spilling like steam—accusations, explanations, defenses—until something inside whispered, *Enough*.

It wasn't anger; it was the knowing that force never creates peace. I turned, lay on the bed, and chose silence. He emerged bewildered. "What just happened?"

"I'm done," I said gently. "I'm not doing this anymore."

Nothing outside changed. The lens did. I stopped seeing myself as the victim who needed to be heard and began seeing myself as the creator who could choose calm. The air in the room didn't shift; I did—and everything felt lighter.

The Power of One Silent Choice

Choosing not to react doesn't mean you're powerless. It means you've reclaimed authorship.

The nervous system learns from these micro-moments:

I can choose peace, even when invited into chaos.

The Garden and the Mirror

My garden taught me to listen without words. When I tended it—watering, pruning, caring—it flourished. When I ignored it, chaos bloomed.

Plants mirrored my life: growth requires attention; love requires tending. Self-worth blossoms when nurtured, not wished into being. Feeding my own roots gave me energy to give from overflow, not depletion. Perspective is the difference between seeing weeds as problems or as reminders to tend what matters.

The Volcano and the Toe

After surgery in Costa Rica, I stared out the window at a distant mountain (volcano) that rose like a quiet guardian.

Below my waist, my body felt foreign—still, unresponsive—except for one big toe that could faintly twitch. The pain was indescribable; the thought of never walking again, sharper still.

I remembered: "If you have faith the size of a mustard seed, you can move mountains."

Maybe faith wasn't about moving the mountain. Maybe it was about honoring a single toe.

So I brought my focus closer: one breath, one thought, one tiny motion. Each morning, I declared, *"Every day, in every way, my body is healing on a cellular level. Thank you, thank you, thank you."* I cradled my leg with a sheet to stimulate circulation, and I wiggled that toe as a vow. This was a mantra I used over and over and over, believing it was what supported my healing journey. Repetition is the mother of embodiment.

Healing wasn't conquering the impossible; it was recognizing the sacred in the smallest movement. Eight months later, I was walking. Not because the mountain moved; my gaze did. Faith, I learned, is a lens: it lets the smallest motion of belief become a miracle.

Now, what can we build with this?

Micro-Motion, Massive Shift

The brain rewires through repetition of small, believable actions. Celebrating a toe wiggle tells your entire system:
Healing is happening. Keep going.
Faith doesn't ignore reality—it chooses which part of reality to amplify.

The Kaleidoscope of Vision

For years at creativity conferences, I passed around kaleidoscopes. Participants gasped as colors rearranged into new shapes. "The patterns didn't change," I'd say. "The angle did."

That's perception: turn the cylinder, and chaos becomes symmetry, pain becomes purpose, what seemed like breaking becomes rearranging. Turn gently, and beauty appears.

The Surrender

Before the surgery, a word kept whispering: surrender. I didn't understand until I lay in that bed, unable to move. Surrender wasn't defeat—it was trust. It was receiving help when pride wanted control. Fear told me surrender was losing. Love showed me surrender is how we're found.

The Hawk's View: Messages from Above

The hawk, my totem, taught me to zoom out—beyond circumstance, beyond the illusion of control. When I'm tangled in details, I spread invisible wings in my mind and rise. From that height, chaos becomes choreography.

Hawks, in many traditions, carry clarity and vision. When one appears, I pause. Spirit seems to say, "Look higher." Nature speaks—animals, feathers, clouds, the rhythm of waves. Some call it coincidence; I call it communication. As above, so below: the wind that carries the hawk carries our prayers. Each time I forget, I look up and remember: the same air that carries the hawk carries me.

Symbol as Language

The soul often understands pictures faster than paragraphs.
A hawk, a feather, a cloud pattern—these can act as visual affirmations: *You're guided. Zoom out. Trust the larger pattern.*

The Hill and the Horse

Seven months pregnant, I slid off my first horse, CD, on a hill. Belly round, reins loose, the saddle looked impossibly high—until CD stepped sideways on her own, positioning herself so I could mount with ease.

It was as if she whispered, "Shift your position, and what feels impossible becomes effortless."

Horses mirror energy: they respond to our nervous system, not our words. Alignment isn't forcing movement from life; it's moving with life.

The Mind Mosaic Clarity Tool™: The Story Beneath the Story

The Tranquil SOULutions Mind Mosaic Clarity Tool™ grew from this truth: What we perceive isn't always what is—it's what we believe.

We look through filters—old hurts, inherited fears, cultural scripts. The Mind Mosaic invites a pause to ask, "Is this true, or is this a story I'm telling myself?" When we step outside the narrative, we become the observer. From there, clarity emerges.

Perception gives us the story. Perspective gives us wisdom. Time and again, a client begins with a "problem," and ends up seeing a pattern. The answer was living in the question. You can watch their breaths deepen as their eyes brighten: *I remember who I am.*

The Mind Mosaic isn't just a tool—it's a mirror of awakening. We are both the artist and the canvas. Choose to see differently, and the image rearranges into beauty.

Spiral Steps — Seeing Through New Eyes

- **Pause & Pivot:** When emotion flares, breathe and ask, *What else could this mean?*
- **Nurture the Garden:** Which part of your life is asking for tending, not fixing?
- **Shift the Lens:** Turn the inner kaleidoscope—name one new possibility you hadn't considered.
- **Find Higher Ground:** Like CD, reposition. Change rooms, posture, or company—notice how effort eases.
- **Zoom Out:** Rise like the hawk to love's altitude; look for patterns, not blame.

- **Write the New Story:** Close your day by reframing one challenge into a lesson. That's the moment you Spiral Up.

Closing Reflection: The Mirror and the Mountain

Life always reflects the lens we use. Through fear, we see barriers. Through faith, we see bridges. Through gratitude, everything becomes a gift.

Sometimes the mountain is real. Other times, it's a molehill magnified by a frightened mind.

Either way, the climb is the same: one breath, one shift, one new perspective at a time.

What can you build with this?

Perhaps a gentler story about who you've been—and who you're becoming. Perspective doesn't erase the mountain; it reminds you that you were always meant to climb it. And with each step, you spiral higher—not away from life, but deeper into it.

"The mountain doesn't have to move for the view to change. Sometimes the miracle is in the shift of the gaze." — **Karen Rudolf**

CHAPTER 8

When Lightning Strikes: Becoming the Light

"When fear dissolves, faith becomes illumination."
— **Karen Rudolf**

Bridge – From Fear to Faith

Perspective teaches us to see differently; embodiment asks us to live differently.

What I had once viewed from the hawk's altitude, I was now being asked to live on the ground—raw, human, trembling in the face of love and loss.

For years, fear ruled my every choice. It froze creation before it could begin, building invisible fences around possibility. I attempted to think my way through what only the heart could feel. The tighter I planned, the tighter the spiral became.

The shift began when I started catching my own words—hearing when they came from lack, doubt, or *I can't*. Each time I softened my language, I softened my life. Each time I chose faith instead of fear, the universe answered with grace.

It wasn't overnight. It was practice—*Cancel. Delete. Reframe.* Over and over, until the vibration of my voice matched the vibration of my heart. Those moments of courage became my training ground for the deepest act of surrender yet.

Fear → Faith

Fear contracts the nervous system.
Faith expands it.
Your biology responds before your mind does.
This is why one small shift in language can feel like a doorway yanked open.

The Goodbye

Some moments remind us how fragile life truly is. We plan, prepare, and dream, and nothing guarantees another sunrise.

Yesterday was one of those moments.

The sun hung high and merciless, the air heavy with stillness. Truman's coat shimmered in broken patches of light. As I brushed his neck, I felt both strength and exhaustion—the steady rhythm of a heartbeat slowing into surrender.

He lifted his head when he saw me, a flicker of his old mischief still alive. I wished he could run one last time, mane wild against the wind— love, real love, sometimes means letting go.

The vet's voice was gentle. "It might be time."

A stone lodged in my chest. There is no such thing as ready.

Truman nudged my hand, reminding me of the promise I'd made after the lightning strike—that I would never let him suffer.

I fed him one last carrot, whispered into his mane, "Thank you for choosing us. You made such a difference in our lives. You're safe, and I love you."

The first injection came—peaceful sedation. His head sank heavily against my shoulder. The second followed—soft, final. He folded gracefully to the earth as if bowing to life itself.

And then, silence. A stillness so pure it cracked me open.

I couldn't watch the burial. My body knew it couldn't bear it. Instead, I walked toward the sea—the place where endings become beginnings.

The Body Knows

The body often understands before the mind does.
Grief lives first in the chest, then in the throat, then in the breath.
Honor those signals—they guide you toward what's most compassionate for your heart.

The Sign

The horizon shimmered as the sun began to set. I whispered a prayer for a sign, something to tell me he was free.

The clouds shifted, and there he was—his image etched in gold: a horse in repose, one hoof extended toward me. Light radiated beneath the cloud like wings.

The ache eased. I knew he was home.

The Message in the Lightning

Years earlier, during a personal-growth seminar, I had been asked, "Who are you 'being' in the world?" Without hesitation, the word *Love* spilled out.

When lightning struck Truman, Reverend Alma asked if I'd looked up its meaning. I told her I didn't need to. I already knew. Lightning is illumination—Spirit's fierce reminder to become light. A "Light Bearer," a "Messenger." And that is exactly what I stepped into.

That day on the beach, I realized the lesson had come full circle. Lightning had once seared fear into me; now it etched grace. Love was never meant to be contained—it expands, transforms, travels beyond us like light after the storm.

Truman had been that light. He taught patience, compassion, and trust. He showed me that healing isn't about holding on—it's about allowing: allowing endings, allowing emotion, allowing love to evolve.

Pain and beauty can live in the same breath. When we resist, we suffer. When we surrender, we spiral upward into peace.

Pain is inevitable; suffering is the story we add to it. I could have clung to guilt, but instead I chose to keep my promise: to let love—not fear—lead.

Love doesn't end with goodbye. It reshapes itself into memory, gratitude, and light. Sometimes it even paints itself across the clouds to remind us: we never truly lose what we've loved—we simply learn to see it differently.

Truly, I asked myself, ***What can I build with this?***

Lightning as Metaphor

Scientifically, lightning equalizes imbalance.
Spiritually, illumination comes when something inside us needs clearing.
What looks violent is often a realignment of energy.

Integration — Coming Home to Love

Grief changes its form over time. What begins as raw ache softens into reverence.

I still glance toward the pasture expecting to see him there, tail flicking, eyes bright. Now I feel presence instead of pain—his energy woven through sunlight, through waves, through every client who rediscovers their own light after a storm.

Each goodbye life has asked of me has become an invitation to live more fully *now*. To speak love aloud. To tell people they matter while they're still here to hear it. To stop waiting for perfect moments and honor the one unfolding.

Letting go isn't the end of connection; it's deepening. When we release with love, we become conduits of it—light in motion. Lightning once startled me awake; now it reminds me that illumination is born from intensity. Even the sharpest pain can break us open to greater love.

Grief as Expansion

Grief is not a sign love ends.
It is a sign love is evolving.
Healing happens when we allow that evolution to move through us without resistance.

Spiral Steps — Reflections for Your Own Journey

Take a quiet breath. Let these prompts meet you where you are:

- **The Promise** – Recall a vow of love you once made—to yourself or another. How might you renew it today?
- **The Release** – Where are you being asked to let go with grace instead of resistance?
- **The Light** – Remember a "lightning-strike" moment—sudden insight born of upheaval. What truth did it reveal?

- **The Choice** – Can you see the difference between pain (what happens) and suffering (the story about it)? How might choosing peace reshape this moment?
- **The Presence** – What single act of being fully present—today, right now—reminds you that life is fragile, yet sacred?

Let your answers unfold gently.

They are sparks lighting your own way home.

What will you build with this?

Closing Reflection

As the sun slid beneath the horizon, a hush fell over the water—an exhale from the day itself.

I stood barefoot in the sand, the last shimmer of gold dissolving into sea and sky, and felt stillness settle inside me.

The world hadn't ended; it had shifted form. Every ending is a beginning wrapped in a different light.

Truman's spirit hadn't vanished—it had merged with everything bright and alive around me.

And in that knowing, I found quiet courage to live wide open—to greet each sunrise as both gift and teacher.

The storms will still come. The lightning will still strike. And each flash now reminds me that even in our fiercest losses, we are never separate from love, only invited to become more of it.

CHAPTER 9

The Alchemy of the Heart: Coming Home to Love

"Gratitude is the quiet alchemy that turns what we have into enough." — **Karen Rudolf**

The Heart's Alchemy

There are moments when the heart cracks open—not to break us, but to let light in. Gratitude, forgiveness, and compassion are the fires through which love refines itself.

This is the alchemy of the heart: where pain transforms into wisdom, and loss reveals the path home to self.

Heart Alchemy

Alchemy is transformation through presence.
The heart doesn't erase what happened;
it **reinterprets** it through love.

Gratitude — The Language of the Soul

After my surgery in Costa Rica, words were few and gestures were everything. Most of the hospital staff didn't speak English, and I didn't speak Spanish. So we spoke the universal language—kindness.

One aide embodied it fully. One afternoon, he entered my room, radiant with joy, eager to tell me—through a translation app—that he had gone to church and prayed for me. His compassion brought me to tears.

On the day of my discharge, he wheeled me to the door. Before I could speak, he reached for my hand. Our eyes met, our tears mirrored—and gratitude became fluent between us.

That moment taught me something profound: Gratitude isn't something we say; it's something we *become*. It flows between souls that recognize each other in love, no matter the barrier of words.

Since that day, I've seen gratitude as a living prayer. Every "thank you" vibrates through the universe as acknowledgment of the sacred. It's not reserved for abundance—it's the bridge that carries us through when life feels bare.

I give thanks for the storms, the teachers, and every hand that reached toward me when I couldn't reach back.

And I give thanks for Reverend Alma, who reminded me that grace is not earned—it's allowed.

Gratitude keeps the heart open to allow it.

Gratitude as Frequency

Gratitude shifts the nervous system from survival into safety.

In that safety, insight, healing, and intuition become easier to access. It's not spiritual bypass—it's spiritual *stabilizing.*

Forgiveness — The Freedom Within

Forgiveness is the quiet revolution of the soul. It doesn't excuse the harm or erase the lesson—it frees us from carrying it. Forgiveness begins where blame ends.

When my marriage ended, I eventually found peace in forgiving both my former husband and his partner. At first, it felt impossible—how could I release something that had cut so deep?
The answer was that forgiveness wasn't for them. It was for me.

Unforgiveness is a chain that tethers us to the past. When we release it, we reclaim our energy.

And perhaps the hardest forgiveness of all was forgiving myself— for staying too long, for trusting too easily, for not seeing sooner.

I used to say, *"I should have known better."* Now I know that every choice was a teacher, every mistake a sacred detour toward wisdom. Forgiving myself wasn't indulgence—it was liberation.

The Lesson Behind the Loss

Not long after selling my marital home, I hired a man from Ireland who claimed to be a spiritual and business coach. He spoke with confidence and conviction—the kind that sounds like truth.

Vulnerable and hopeful, I trusted him. I sent the money. And he disappeared.

When friends asked how I could be so calm, I said, "I can't cry over spilled milk. This is a lesson I'll never forget." And I haven't. That experience became one of my greatest teachers.

It taught me that discernment is love in action. Those boundaries are spiritual protection. That faith without wisdom is only wishful thinking.

Now I sense misalignment long before it reaches my door. Not from fear—rather from presence.

Because when you know yourself, deception loses its power.

I've forgiven him completely. He returned me to my intuition—a costly, priceless lesson.

Forgiveness means forgiving forever—no longer holding another hostage for what they did or didn't do.

That's the true alchemy of forgiveness: transforming deception into discernment, and pain into power.

I certainly learned and built upon this lesson well!

Discernment as Self-Love

Discernment isn't mistrust; it's refined trust.
It says: I trust myself enough to choose what's aligned and release what isn't.

Compassion — The Pulse of Connection

Compassion is the bridge between empathy and action. It lets us sit with another's pain without needing to fix it.

As the host of *The Awakening Potential Show,* I listen to people's stories—of heartbreak, breakthrough, reinvention—and each time I'm reminded how universal our struggles truly are.

We may walk different paths, still, our hearts beat to the same rhythm of longing and love.

Compassion isn't something we *give*. It's something we *remember* within ourselves—reflected through another's story. It invites understanding without judgment and love without conditions.

It's not about helping; it's about seeing. Holding space. Letting the truth unfold.

Opinions — The Uninvited Guests of the Heart

With compassion comes discernment. And one of the hardest lessons I've learned is that not every voice deserves a seat at your inner table.

For years, I was swayed by others' opinions—about who I should be, how I should live, and what "healing" should look like. I mistook unsolicited advice for truth. Yet, opinions are projections, not prophecies.

They reveal more about the speaker's beliefs than about your reality. Unless we've asked for them—and are open to receiving—they hold no real weight.

When we live for approval, we trade authenticity for acceptance. When we listen inwardly, opinions become information rather than instruction.

Now I remind myself often: *Not every comment requires a comeback. Not every opinion deserves an answer.*

True compassion allows others their view—without needing to absorb it. That's balance: staying open-hearted without being overexposed. Opinions swirl like wind, but peace belongs to the rooted.

What can you build with this knowledge?

Guarding the Inner Table

You are allowed to choose who gets a "vote" in your life.
Your heart is a sacred space, not a public forum.

Self-Love and Responsibility — The Return Home

For years, I lived as a people-pleaser—believing my worth was measured by what I did for others. Learning to love myself meant learning to listen to myself.

Boundaries became blessings. Journaling became a mirror. Stillness became medicine.

Self-love isn't vanity—it's vibrational hygiene. It's how we tend our energy so what flows from us is clean, kind, and intentional. When we take responsibility for our vibration, we stop reacting and begin responding.

Freedom lives on the other side of responsibility. When we own our choices, words, and energy, we stop feeling trapped by circumstance. Mistakes become messages. Falling becomes flight.

Failure becomes feedback.

Compassion is toward self first and foremost; *what can you build with this?*

The Tears That Freed Me

While recovering in the Costa Rican hospital, I received word that Apache—one of our rescue horses—had passed.

I'd been stoic through physical pain, but that news broke something open. Tears came raw and relentless—not just for Apache, but for everything: the loss, the exhaustion, the surrender. I cried until I felt hollow, then light.

Grief had carved out space for grace. In that moment, I understood: Gratitude opens the heart.

Forgiveness clears it. Compassion fills it again with light.

Integration — Coming Home to Love

Love, in its truest form, isn't something we find—it's something we remember. Every act of gratitude, forgiveness, and compassion brings us closer to that remembrance.

We don't need to be fixed—only witnessed.
We are whole, even in our healing.
We are worthy, even in our wounds.
We are loved, even when we forget how to love ourselves.

Coming home to love is courage—the courage to face what was, to release what no longer serves, and to open again with tenderness.
That's freedom.
That's peace.
That's the alchemy of the heart.

Coming Home to Self

Coming home to self isn't about discovering who you are—it's about remembering who you've always been beneath the noise and roles.

For years, I attempted to earn love by doing: caring, managing, being "the strong one." And when I finally turned inward, I realized love was never missing. I had simply been standing outside my own door.

Self-love is not a luxury; it's a responsibility. It means honoring your truth even when it's inconvenient. It means forgiving yourself for every moment you forgot your worth. It means trusting your inner rhythm more than the world's noise.

Peace doesn't come from what you fix—it comes from what you finally accept. And in that stillness, you realize: you are your own safe place. When we come home to ourselves, we stop chasing love. We *become* it.

Spiral Steps — Reflections for Your Own Heart

- **Gratitude Practice:** Each night, name three moments that brought light to your day. Let "thank you" be your quiet prayer.
- **Forgiveness Flow:** Write a letter of forgiveness—to another and to yourself. You don't have to send it; just release it.
- **Compassion Check-In:** Notice where you can replace judgment with curiosity.
- **Responsibility Reset:** Ask, How can I respond with grace rather than reaction?
- **Coming Home:** Sit in silence, hand over heart. Whisper, '*I AM whole. I AM love. I AM home.*'

Closing Reflection

The heart is the true alchemist. It takes everything we've ever experienced—the joy, the pain, the loss, the love—and distills it into wisdom.

When we live from that place, even the hardest lessons become sacred. Because love, once remembered, never leaves. It becomes who we are.

And that, above all, is the greatest miracle of all—coming home to love.

"When I return to gratitude, I return to myself. And in that homecoming, everything becomes enough." — **Karen Rudolf**

CHAPTER 10

Spiraling Up – The Embodied Manifestation

Become Someone who Commands Your Light!

"I don't ask, I command. Not by wish, by demand.
I don't ask, I expand."
— Good Vibes Tribe 11:11 (song)

The Call of Confirmation

When the lyrics hit me, the universe wasn't whispering anymore — it was *declaring*:

"You're ready."

What if the confirmation you're waiting for has already arrived?

The timing wasn't random.
The message wasn't accidental.
This was resonance meeting embodiment.

For the first time, I didn't just *believe* I could manifest.

I was *living* as the woman who manifests by being.

There are no coincidences—only confirmations. The universe speaks in whispers, in rhythms, in songs that find us exactly when our souls are ready to hear them.

When a friend sent me that song out of the blue, its message struck every chord within me. I smiled because I knew: this was no random tune. It was the universe echoing what I had finally come to embody—

I don't ask. I command.
I don't beg. I believe.
I don't chase. I align.

Of commanding—not with ego, but with embodied truth.

Manifestation had stopped being a "tool" and had become the natural exhale of who I was becoming.

And the universe responded in kind:

"She finally understands."
"She finally remembers."
"Now watch what unfolds."

What if the signs you're looking for only appear once you've become ready to receive them?

I don't ask. I command...

The Embodiment Map: Sassy–Classy–Badassy™

To command your light without forcing, I return to three lived energies:

- **Sassy:** the spark of courage — the "yes" that expands you.
- **Classy:** the refinement of grace — alignment over effort.
- **Badassy:** the embodiment of freedom — movement, action, and follow-through.

Sassy is the Harmony, Classy is the Purpose, and Badassy is the Mastery.

The Butterfly Within

Butterflies have always been messengers in my life—gentle, patient reminders that transformation isn't instant; it's alchemical.

The caterpillar doesn't try to become a butterfly. It dissolves within its cocoon, surrendering to something greater moving through it. That surrender is trust in motion.

Years ago, I asked the universe for a sign—a butterfly. I wanted proof that manifestation worked, that my thoughts mattered. The next morning, a small yellow butterfly appeared on my lanai.

Coincidence, I told myself.

But then came more: a white one on my car mirror, another on the door handle, a butterfly-shaped bench on my walk, a red fabric butterfly above a friend's sink. By day's end, the skeptic in me had surrendered.

The universe had heard me—because I was finally listening. That simple manifestation cracked something open. I realized I was always manifesting—my focus, my faith, even my fears.

The question became: *What frequency am I feeding?*

Living the Spiral of Creation

Manifestation isn't magic—it's movement. It's the spiral of awareness that begins with intention, expands through trust, and anchors through aligned action, through expansion. It's not linear. It's rhythmic, like a song.

I believe gratitude is the baseline, faith is the melody, and action is the rhythm that makes the music and keeps it alive.

When I said *yes* to life, life says yes back—again and again.

One yes led to another—Les Brown collaborations, best-seller banners, a Nasdaq billboard, even two feature films. Each yes was a ripple of the last—a thread of trust weaving miracles through my life.

What if Manifestation isn't about controlling *how*, rather about being available? Each yes created ripples that built bridges to the next chapter of my life.

Pause. Ask yourself, ***What can I build with the ripples?***

Lessons in Trust: The House, the Dolphin, and the Kitten

After my divorce, I told the realtor I wanted *trees, a fireplace, a gas stove, and a nearby water source.*
He laughed. "You're in Florida. Good luck."

Days later, I found a small home—gas stove, a fireplace, trees all around, and a waterway just beyond the yard. Four for four. That's not a coincidence. That's clarity made visible.

Soon after, my daughter wished to see her dolphin friend once more before moving away.

No dolphins appeared—until she set her intention. Moments later, the dolphin surfaced at her feet. Minutes later, she whispered, *"I want to find a kitten."* An hour later, a two-week-old kitten appeared at the window of my brother's house.

When desire meets alignment, the universe moves quickly.

The universe is always listening. *The only question is: Are we speaking the language of belief or doubt?* **What can we build with this?**

The Grandfather's Lesson

When I once asked my grandfather if he had regrets, he said the only dream my grandmother had was to visit Israel. He always promised, *"When I retire, we'll go."* She passed before that day came.

That moment etched a vow in me: *Don't wait for later. Live your yes now.* Manifestation begins in motion, not in "someday."

What can we build with this?

Commanding Frequency

There's a hum beneath manifestation—a vibration that feels electric when I'm aligned.

It isn't anxious; it's *alive.*

When I command frequency, every cell lights up and says, *"Yes, we remember."* That's the flow—clarity over chatter, communion over control.

Command is not force. It is conviction without fear.

Gratitude fuels it.
Love sustains it.

Confidence amplifies it.
And yes—it takes action.

Faith and trust aren't about sitting back and hoping; they're about walking forward and trusting the next stone will rise to meet your foot.

You get to **choose what to build with that!**

The Spiral Practices

Morning – Command the Day

Before my feet touch the floor, I name three new things I'm grateful for.
I declare: *"I am being ___."*
I write: *By (date), I have manifested ___ and I feel ___."*
Then I choose three aligned actions.

Who are you deciding to be today?

Daytime – Stay in Motion

Walk. Dance. Stretch. Energy in motion stays in creation.
When life feels heavy, I pause, tap my heart three times, and breathe the word *peace, peace, peace.*

Evening – Close the Loop

Reflect on what worked, what was learned, and what was noticed.
Celebrate every win—a kitchen dance counts.

Celebration is gratitude in motion.

Recommit not from fixing rather from expanding.

The Spiral Truth

Manifestation isn't about asking for what you lack—it's remembering who you are. It's gratitude meeting action, energy becoming form through love.

The woman I once was lived in fear and silenced her intuition to keep the peace. The woman I am now *commands* peace. She moves with grace, dances with faith, and breathes gratitude as prayer. She has spiraled through storms to become their calm.

You are both the soil and the light–the cocoon and the wings–the butterfly emerging from your own becoming in motion.

Who are you becoming as you spiral upward?

Every thought, every yes, every act of gratitude is a seed. What you plant in faith, you harvest in form.

Integration — Living as Light

Every experience—every heartbreak, every healing, every surrender—is part of the divine choreography of becoming.

The spiral never ends; it simply expands. Each turn brings us to a higher octave of remembering that manifestation isn't something we do—it's what we *are*.

You are the frequency.
You are the prayer answered.
You are the evidence of what happens when faith meets form.

Once, I searched for signs that I was guided. Now, I *am* the sign. Every smile, every courageous yes, ripples light for someone else finding their way.

That is *Spiraling Up*—living as grace, gratitude, and grounded faith.

When we live from the center of our spiral, we stop asking *Why me?* and start asking *What is this awakening within me?*

From that center—calm, steady, luminous—we radiate.

What can I build with this?

The Universal Symphony

We are all instruments in the same divine orchestra. When we tune to gratitude, compassion, and faith, we become harmony itself.

You don't have to be fearless to be free—only willing. Every act of gratitude is a note, every forgiveness a rest, every leap of faith a crescendo. You are not separate from the music; *you are its rhythm.*

Build as your Powerful Self! Trust you!

Embodying the Spiral

To live this way is to practice presence, not perfection. Alignment—not effort—is the true currency of success.

When you live as your own light, manifestation becomes natural. It's not about getting what you want rather *becoming who you are.*

The butterfly never forces its wings open. It simply allows the light to transform.

What becomes possible when you stop forcing and start allowing?

Spiral Steps — Living Manifestation

- **Command Your Morning:** Breathe gratitude and declare, *"I am the light I've been waiting for."*

- **Align with Action:** Choose the yes that expands you.
- **Move Energy:** Walk, dance, breathe—motion is manifestation.
- **Return to Peace:** Tap your heart and whisper, *"I trust."*
- **Close the Day:** List what went well and celebrate your courage to live awake.

What you celebrate, you invite more of.

When you celebrate, you multiply.

Closing Reflection — The Light You Are

As I look back, I see not a path of perfection rather of presence—faith, forgiveness, and fearless becoming.

Every storm refined me.
Every stillness restored me.
Every "no" redirected me to a greater yes.

Through it all, one truth remains:

You are a miracle.
You are the manifestation.
You are the light you once prayed to find.

As you step beyond this page, remember–the *spiral* doesn't end, only expands.

Keep rising.
Keep expanding.
Keep shining.

Because the more you remember your own light,
the brighter the world becomes through you.

"Music has always been my prayer in motion —the language of gratitude, healing, and embodiment. My hope is that these songs remind you that you, too, can rise, dance, and spiral up — again and again." — **Karen Rudolf**

The Music of Becoming

A Soundtrack for Spiraling Up

---

*"Every song is a step in the spiral — lifting,
expanding, and embodying who we are becoming."*
— **Karen Rudolf**

Music has scored every chapter of my life — from the quiet ache of surrender to the radiant rise of becoming. These songs aren't just melodies; they're mile markers. They carried me, lifted me, cracked me open, and rebuilt me in rhythm with my awakening.

Think of this as your sonic spiral — a way to feel every step more deeply, remembering that your healing, your growth, and your expansion have always had a soundtrack.

Which songs are speaking to the person you're becoming — not the one you're leaving behind?

PART I – THE BEGINNING: Songs That Lifted Me

(Faith · Healing · Hope Rising)

These were the anthems that held me when I wasn't ready to hold myself.
They reminded me that surrender isn't defeat — it's devotion.
It's the moment we soften enough for grace to enter.

The early days of my spiral were marked by raw honesty, whispered prayers, and the quiet rebuilding of trust. These songs helped me breathe again when life felt heavy. They were the hands beneath my wings before I remembered I had them.

Core Feelings: Faith, Surrender, Trust, Peace, Grace

Songs:

- Overwhelmed – Big Daddy Weave
- Testify to Love – Avalon
- Never Alone (Radio Remix) – BarlowGirl
- It Is Well (Live) – Bethel Music & Kristene DiMarco
- Burning Lights – Chris Tomlin
- Lay Me Down – Chris Tomlin
- Indescribable – Chris Tomlin
- I Am – Crowder
- Rise – Danny Gokey
- Come to the Altar (Live) – Elevation Worship
- Believe – Fearless Soul
- Thy Will – Hillary Scott & The Scott Family
- Oceans (Where Feet May Fail) – Hillsong UNITED
- Remind Me Who I Am – Jason Gray
- Halleluya – Lawrence Collins Band
- Happy – Leona Lewis
- Hero – Mariah Carey
- You Gotta Believe – Natalie Brown
- Fear Is a Liar – Zach Williams
- Lean on Me – Bill Withers
- Surrender – Natalie Taylor

What if surrender is the soul's way of saying, "I'm ready to rise"?

Reflection Prompts:

- Which of these songs brings you back to your faith or center when life feels uncertain?
- What lyrics remind you that surrender is not weakness, but strength?
- Where in your life are you being asked to soften instead of struggle?

PART II – THE RISE: Songs That Strengthened Me

(Courage · Empowerment · Becoming)

As I spiraled upward, these songs became my fuel. They reminded me that *courage isn't loud — it's consistent.*
Healing isn't linear — it's rhythmic. And self-worth isn't found — it's reclaimed.

This was the season where I stopped apologizing for existing.
Stopped shrinking.
Stopped settling.
These songs met me in the moment *I chose myself — fiercely, vulnerably, entirely.*

As your spiral ascends, these tracks reflected self-acceptance, resilience, and reclaiming your power.

Core Feelings: Courage, Confidence, Healing, Empowerment

Songs:

- Wings of Light – Girls, Party Tyme
- Broken Wings – Mr. Mister
- Got It in You – BANNERS

- I'm Not Okay – Jelly Roll
- Don't Stop Believin' – Journey
- You Got This – Love & The Outcome
- You Make Me Feel – Aretha Franklin
- I Want to Know What Love Is – Foreigner
- Rise Up – Andra Day
- Love Myself – Olivia O'Brien
- Scars to Your Beautiful – Alessia Cara
- Unbreakable – Janelle Monáe / Kelly Clarkson
- You Will Be Found – Ben Platt
- Believer – Lea Michele
- The Climb – Miley Cyrus
- You Say – Lauren Daigle
- Man in the Mirror – Michael Jackson
- Out of the Ashes – LA Samuel
- The Light – Adam Lambert
- Already Enough – Fearless Soul & Rachael Schroeder
- Unstoppable – Sia
- Brand New Me – Alicia Keys
- Girl on Fire – Alicia Keys
- Superwoman – Alicia Keys
- Wake Me Up – Avicii
- Fearless – Jasmine Murray
- Good to Be Alive – Jason Gray
- Love My Life – Robbie Williams
- The Mountain – Faouzia
- Legends Are Made – Sam Tinnesz
- Born for This – The Score
- The Champion – Carrie Underwood
- Warrior – Demi Lovato

Which version of you rises when the music gets louder?

Reflection Prompts:

- Which song makes you feel unstoppable?
- When have you turned fear into faith or courage into clarity?
- What anthem mirrors the woman you're claiming now?

PART III – THE EMBODIED LIGHT: Songs That Became Me

(Freedom · Joy · Gratitude · Expansion)

The anthems of arrival — music that reflects your embodied, radiant, confident self.

These are not just songs I listened to —
they are songs I *became.*

They celebrate the woman who rose from her own ashes.
The woman who leads with heart and clarity.
The woman who commands her life with gratitude as her frequency and joy as her compass.

This is the music of embodiment — the soundtrack of living as your own light.

Core Feelings: Joy, Freedom, Gratitude, Radiance, Celebration

Songs:

- Hall of Fame – The Script
- Moments We Live For – In Paradise
- The Work – Rob Riccardo
- Capital Letters – Hailee Steinfeld
- Human – Rag'n'Bone Man / Roman Mulier

- Let It Go – Dani Corbalan
- I Was Here – Beyoncé
- I Lived – OneRepublic
- Thankful – Celine Dion
- Grateful – Rita Ora
- Thank You for Everything – Jason Gray
- Receive – Fia
- Just Like Magic – Ariana Grande
- Power Is You – Mi Casa & Pascal Morais
- Broken & Beautiful – Kelly Clarkson
- Chasing Dreams – GoodLuck
- On Top of the World – Imagine Dragons
- Me Too – Meghan Trainor
- Better When I'm Dancin' – Meghan Trainor
- Express Yourself – Madonna
- Awake My Soul – Mumford & Sons
- Courage to Change – Sia
- Just Be You – Sadie Robertson
- Hearts Mystery – Nick Barber
- Brave – Sara Bareilles

When did joy stop being a visitor and start becoming your home?

Reflection Prompts:

- Which of these songs embodies your frequency now?
- How does your heart move when you listen to them?
- Which melody feels like your future self speaking?

Closing Invitation

This soundtrack is a living, breathing extension of your evolution.
Return to it whenever you forget how far you've come —
or when you're ready to rise again.
Which song will you choose to spiral into next?

What can you build with this?

The Ripple Continues

"The bridge between ordinary and extraordinary is built with small steps of change and big leaps of faith." **— Karen Rudolf**

The spiral never really ends; it only widens.

Every lesson we live becomes part of a greater pattern—each choice, each healing, each act of courage sending ripples far beyond what we can see. When I look back at my own journey, I see how every story I've shared—whether written, spoken, or lived—has been one of those ripples, moving outward in ever-widening circles of light.

It began with ***5 Ways to Create a Ripple,*** my first solo book and the seed of everything that followed—a reminder that one act of courage can create waves of change. Since then, I've had the privilege of contributing to multiple collaborative books, each marking a new level of awareness and embodiment. Together, they became a chronicle of growth: faith rediscovered, wellness redefined, and the courage to lead with authenticity.

Those collaborations weren't just collections of stories—they were communities of hearts, women and men rising together through shared purpose. Each project invited me to peel back another layer of self, to speak more vulnerably, to trust the ripple even when I couldn't see where it would land.

In writing those chapters, I found my voice.
In connecting with others, I found my power.
And in witnessing our collective transformation, I found proof that healing is never meant to happen alone. Healing becomes a choice daily to become the best version of yourself, a lifestyle I get to choose, *not* what happened to me.

All those threads lead here—to **Spiraling Up**.

This book is a collection of integrations so many of the lessons I've lived; the moment where awareness became embodiment, and embodiment became service. It's the realization that the spiral is not about reaching a destination—it's about becoming more present with every turn.

I think often of Scamper and Truman, my four-legged messengers, and how their lightning-lit paths taught me that love never truly ends—it simply changes form. The same is true for our growth. Each chapter of life gives way to another, each ending births a beginning, and each healed heart becomes a beacon for others still finding their way.

As my work evolved, **Mind Mosaic™** emerged—a living bridge between reflection and transformation, teaching that clarity isn't something we chase; it's something we reveal. One pattern at a time. One breath at a time. One spiral at a time.

My hope is that ***Spiraling Up*** reaches you exactly where you are and supports you to rise into who you are becoming. ***Command Your Life!*** You get to choose.

You are part of this ripple now.

Your courage, your reflections, your willingness to live what you've learned—these are what keep the spiral alive. Together, we create a wave of awareness, compassion, and light that moves through the world one awakened soul at a time.

So when life circles back, and you find yourself facing something familiar, remember this: it isn't a setback—it's an invitation. A call to embody what you've learned, to stand taller in your truth, to love more deeply than before.

Because the spiral is never about falling.
It's about rising—again and again—into the light of who you truly are infinitely!

In sacred geometry, a spiral never returns to the same point—it expands. So do you.

Every familiar moment is not a repeat... It's an opportunity to rise at a higher frequency.

A Final Invitation

When you close this book, your next chapter begins.
Let every breath, every choice, every word be an upward turn in your own spiral.

Final Blessing

Spiraling Up: The Light You Command!

May your spiral always lead you home—to love, to truth, and to the light within.

Rise again and again—gracefully, boldly, and unapologetically—

for you are the spiral in motion, a ripple in the great rhythm of becoming.

— Karen Rudolf
Founder of Tranquil SOULutions™
Author | Speaker | Catalyst for Change / Creator of the Mind Mosaic Clarity Tool ™

The Spiral Creed

A Declaration of Becoming

I am the light I once searched for.
The whisper I once prayed to hear.
The stillness I once feared to enter.

I have shed the skin of who I was,
honored the ache of my own becoming,
and risen, again and again, through love's unfolding.

I am not here to fix what was never broken.
I am here to remember what has always been whole.

I speak life into being.
I move as gratitude: embodied.
I trust the timing of all things.
I live as the bridge between heaven and earth—
as above, so below.

I am both the storm and the calm after it,
the lightning and the light it leaves behind.
I am the butterfly,
born of surrender, sustained by faith,
and carried by grace into the next horizon.

I no longer ask.
I no longer chase.
I no longer wait.
I *command*, because I am.

This is my spiral—
ever upward, ever open, ever becoming.

And as I rise,
I awaken potential in others to rise too.

— Karen Rudolf, Tranquil SOULutions™

<u>ACKNOWLEDGMENTS</u>

To Every Soul Who Walked With Me

To all who have touched my path, shaped my journey, cracked me open, and lifted me higher—I am profoundly grateful.

To my daughters, whose laughter, honesty, and fierce love have been both mirror and compass. You have taught me more about courage, grace, and truth than any book or teacher ever could.

To my four-legged messengers—Scamper, Truman, and the animals who have whispered wisdom through breath and presence. You reminded me that healing is often wordless and that love speaks in energy.

To my mentors, teachers, and spiritual guides who believed in my voice long before I learned to trust it. Thank you for teaching me that intuition is a birthright and that transformation lives in the everyday moments of choosing again.

To every collaborator, co-author, and visionary woman whose stories have intertwined with mine—your courage created ripples that reached far beyond the pages. Each project was not merely a book, rather a community, a rising, a remembering.

To the countless clients, friends, and souls who have sat with me in moments of breakthrough and vulnerability—your willingness to awaken has inspired my own. Every session, every conversation, and every tear shed and truth spoken have woven themselves into this spiral.

And to you—my reader—thank you for trusting these words, trusting your journey, and trusting the whisper within you. You are now part of this ripple, part of the rising. Your presence here matters more than you know.

May the light you carry continue touching others in ways you may never fully see, but will always be felt.

About the Author

Karen Rudolf is a transformational guide, speaker, and creator of the *Mind Mosaic Clarity Tool™*, known for supporting others in awakening their inner wisdom, releasing old patterns, and rising into lives of intention, self-compassion, and freedom. With her signature blend of intuition, emotional intelligence, trauma-informed practices, and neuroscience-aligned tools, she supports others in shifting from survival mode into empowered, heart-led living.

A contributing author to more than ten international bestselling books, Karen's work centers on supporting people to reclaim their voice, rewrite their story, and reconnect with the truth of who they are. As host of ***The Awakening Potential Show***, she curates soulful conversations that spark clarity, courage, and the kind of insight that lingers long after the episode ends.

Karen is also featured in the upcoming documentaries ***The Art of Manifestation*** and ***The Frequency of Healing*** (2026), where her teachings on energy, presence, and awakening potential are brought to a global audience.

At her core, Karen is a guide who walks the walk — blending compassion with practicality, presence with direction, and wisdom with just the right amount of sass. Her Signature Sassy-Classy-Badassy framework reflects her belief that true transformation isn't about becoming someone new... It's about becoming **more unapologetically you**:

- **Sassy** enough to trust your voice

- **Classy** enough to lead with grace
- **Badassy** enough to take the bold, aligned action your soul keeps whispering about

Karen finds joy in nature, horses, creativity, travel, deep conversations, and the quiet moments that bring life back into harmony. She honors her three daughters as her greatest teachers and credits her beloved horse Truman—her "Catalyst for Change"—for inspiring some of her most profound healing and purpose.

She is available for Stages, and you can explore more of Karen's work and offerings at www.**TranquilSOULutions.com**.

About Tranquil SOULutions™

Tranquil SOULutions™ is Karen's signature ecosystem for heart-centered transformation—a space where science meets spirituality, intuition meets intention, and healing meets empowerment.

Through coaching, courses, speaking, retreats, and the groundbreaking **Mind Mosaic™** digital tool, Tranquil SOULutions™ supports women in dissolving limiting beliefs, clearing emotional patterns, and stepping into a life of harmony, confidence, and authentic expression.

At the heart of the work is a simple truth:
When you align your inner world, your outer world transforms naturally.

About Mind Mosaic™ — A New Way to See Your Inner World

Born from sixteen years of study, practice, and personal awakening, **Mind Mosaic™** is a digital clarity tool designed to reveal patterns, shift perspectives, and illuminate the subconscious stories shaping your life.

It offers a guided inward journey—through reflection, intuition, energetic inquiry, and pattern recognition—leading to insights that transform the way you move through the world.

Mind Mosaic™ is more than a tool. It is a companion, a mirror, a catalyst.

And for many, it becomes the first step to lasting emotional freedom.

About The Butterfly Technique — Transform Through the Pause

Inspired by the natural rhythm of a butterfly's transformation, this simple but powerful three-step method helps you interrupt emotional spirals and return to alignment.

STOP – Pause the reaction.
CHANGE – Shift the narrative or meaning.
SHIFT – Reclaim your energy and choose a new response.

This gentle method mirrors the entire theme of Spiraling Up: small moments of awareness creating profound transformation.

A Final Invitation

Your journey doesn't end here. In fact, it begins now—at the moment where awareness becomes embodiment.

When you breathe slowly...
When you choose differently...
When you speak with intention...
When you trust the rhythm within...

You are spiraling up.

If these pages have supported you, guided you, or awakened something inside you, know this:

**You are ready for the next chapter—
and the spiral will meet you wherever you choose to rise.**

Thank you for walking this path with me.
May your life continue unfolding in harmony, courage, freedom, and truth.

Spiraling Up:
Command Your Light!

Tranquil SOULutions was created by Karen Rudolf for visionary leaders who are done living in push-mode.

This movement exists because high performers don't need more "mindset hacks."
They need capacity restored, clarity reclaimed, and a way to lead from their power — not their pressure.

Spiraling Up is a living practice:
A new way of thinking, speaking, choosing, and creating — where your inner world becomes the place your leadership is sourced from.

This is for you if...

- You've been carrying a lot (and making it look easy).
- You're ready to stop negotiating with your own power.
- You want calm clarity *and* bold action — without burnout.

Start here:

Download the Spiral Up Integration Guide
(7-day capacity reset)
https://karenrudolf.com/spiral-up-7-day-nervous-system-reset

Want support mapping your next step?

Book a 20-minute Spiral Up Mapping Session
https://api.leadconnectorhq.com/widget/bookings/20mindmappingsession

Want community + weekly momentum?

Join The New Paradigm of Leadership™ inside Skool

https://www.skool.com/awakeningpotential-collective-5012/about

QR CODE for all 3 links